Investing in

M000195524

Most higher-education finance literature assumes that students cannot pledge their future earnings to finance their education in a free society. *Investing in Human Capital* challenges that assumption and explores human capital contracts (HCCs) as an alternative mechanism for financing higher education. *Investing in Human Capital* tracks the roots of the idea behind HCCs, discusses the beneficial consequences they would have on students and on higher-education markets, and describes how they can develop in light of the innovations that have taken place in financial markets during the 1980s and 1990s. The book also explores the challenges – ethical and financial – that such instruments face and offers implementation alternatives that can bring about their existence in the context of a national higher-education financing program.

MIGUEL PALACIOS LLERAS is a Fellow at the Batten Institute, Darden School of Business Administration at the University of Virginia. He is the author of several papers on financing human capital and is co-founder of Lumni, a company that manages human capital funds.

Investing in Human Capital

A Capital Markets Approach to Student Funding

MIGUEL PALACIOS LLERAS

CAMBRIDGE
UNIVERSITY PRESS

CAMBRIDGE UNIVERSITY PRESS
Cambridge, New York, Melbourne, Madrid, Cape Town, Singapore, São Paulo

Cambridge University Press
The Edinburgh Building, Cambridge CB2 8RU, UK

Published in the United States of America by Cambridge University Press, New York

www.cambridge.org
Information on this title: www.cambridge.org/9780521828406

First published 2004
This digitally printed version 2007

A catalogue record for this publication is available from the British Library

Library of Congress Cataloguing in Publication data
Palacios, Miguel.
Investing in human capital : a capital markets approach to student funding /
Miguel Palacios Lleras.
        p.   cm.
Includes bibliographical references and index.
ISBN 0 521 82840 6
1. Student loan funds.   2. Education, Higher – Finance.   3. Human capital.   I. Title.
LB2340.P35   2003
378.3´62 – dc21   2003053195

ISBN 978-0-521-82840-6 hardback
ISBN 978-0-521-03952-9 paperback

To those whose
financial situation does not
allow them to develop their
full potential, and
to my parents,
Hugo and Maria Mercedes, who
have continuously made
every effort to
develop mine.

If a nation expects to be ignorant and free in a state of civilization, it expects what never was and never will be.

Thomas Jefferson

Contents

ix

Figures

Tables

Foreword

Labor productivity is fundamental to economic growth, as modeled formally in the literature on endogenous growth. Indeed, with global capital markets and rapid transmission of technology, it can be argued that human capital is more important than ever as a determinant of national economic performance and individual well-being.

Fifty years ago higher education was largely a consumption good for a middle-class elite. In most countries, 5 per cent (or less) of 18-year olds went to university. With technological advance, the demand for highly skilled workers has increased sharply: student and employer demand for tertiary education and training is larger and more diverse than previously, and is repeated, in the sense that people require re-training. As a result, countries today increasingly have mass systems of higher education. A central question, therefore, is how to finance these systems so as to facilitate economic growth and equitable access to higher education. In poorer countries, fiscal capacity is limited; and even in richer countries, public spending is constrained by international competition, which imposes limits to taxation in any one country, and by parallel pressures such as population ageing. Public funding thus needs to be supplemented by private sources.

In principle, private finance could come from family resources, from a student's earnings while a student, from a student's future earnings, from employers, from entrepreneurial activities by universities, and/or from gifts and donations. But many of these sources are less lucrative than they appear at first sight. Family resources can be substantial, but do nothing to improve access for students from poor backgrounds. Earnings during student days are generally small (the USA is exceptional). Employer contributions are also generally small (each employer has an interest in poaching people whose training has been financed by a competitor). Entrepreneurial activities by universities are also likely to be small in many countries (again, the USA is an exception). Gifts, for example through fundraising, are also largely illusory – even in the

USA, large-scale fundraising is successful only for a small number of the best-known universities and is largely irrelevant to other tertiary institutions.

The only remaining option, and the only approach capable of yielding resources on a large scale and in an equitable way, is to facilitate consumption smoothing – i.e. to develop mechanisms which allow people to gain access during their student days to their own future earnings.

Student loans are one way of doing so. However, there are good reasons why the private market has developed loans to buy a house but not loans to finance an educational qualification. The theoretical issue is how to design student loans taking account of constraints parties face in writing and enforcing contracts. The resulting problems include capital market imperfections (the absence of security for loans for human capital) and information problems (for instance, adverse selection) in financial markets. Resolving those issues has taken time.

My own writing has focused on student loans with income-contingent repayments, i.e. repayments in the form of x percent of a person's subsequent earnings until she has paid off the loan; and such arrangements are now in place in several countries including Australia (since 1989), New Zealand (1993), and the UK (1998). In my proposals, students pay an interest rate broadly equal to the risk-free borrowing rate, with repayments collected alongside income tax or social security contributions. In most systems (e.g. in Australia and New Zealand) the loans are publicly funded; but it is possible to bring in private finance either (as in the UK) through the retrospective sale of student debt, or (as in the USA) where students borrow from private sources. In such a system, the loan contract is determined centrally by government and is identical for all borrowers: loans are publicly organised, but may be privately funded, the underlying model having much of the flavor of social insurance.

This book takes as its starting point the original proposal by Milton Friedman to use equity rather than loan finance as the major device for consumption smoothing. In Friedman's original proposal, a student finances her university education by selling the right to x *percent* of her annual earnings. A low-earning student repays less than the cost of her higher education, thus the stakeholder makes a loss; in the case of a high-earnings student, the stakeholder makes a profit.

The book's important new insight is to bring the loan approach and the equity finance approach together into a single analytical framework. As one example, consider what the author calls a human capital contract (HCC), whereby a person obtains the finance for her higher education by selling the right to *x percent* of her earning for *n* years, i.e. equity finance of the sort just described. That contract could be supplemented by a second contract in which the student buys a human capital option (HCO), which insures the graduate against overpaying if she turns out to be high earner. The combination of the HCC and HCO is an income-contingent loan (ICL).

The application of option theory to the finance of higher education is entirely new – finance theory meets ICLs. This is a significant intellectual advance.

As well as being an intellectual advance, the approach also points toward policy innovation. If, as the book argues, equity finance is more suitable to private contracts than loan finance, the combination of an HCC with an HCO enables the private market to provide ICLs based on individualized contracts. This, the book argues, improves efficiency because of the resulting market signals. For example, it would be possible to get a loan on better terms for a more expensive degree with better earnings outcomes than for a cheaper degree with poorer outcomes.

As with any radical idea, there are unresolved issues. The book makes a powerful case for private finance of higher education and for a mechanism that gives market signals. That analysis (and the case for market forces more generally) rests on the assumption that agents are well informed. Though that is, for the most part, the right assumption for higher education, issues remain about how to protect applicants who are not well informed (there are obvious analogies with private pensions – another example of consumption smoothing – where complex, long-term contracts make consumer protection essential). Another issue is whether HCCs are a form of slavery. The author argues that they are not, because what the person pre-commits is a fraction of her future *income* not her future *activities*, and thus retains full freedom over her future course of action. I accept that argument fully but again, only if it is right to assume that students are well informed.

In addition to analytical questions, the idea also raises practical issues. That, however, detracts neither from the idea nor from the analysis. Income contingency was for many years regarded as sound in theory but not capable of implementation. HCCs are an important and powerful idea; and the idea is being tested on a small scale in a number of countries. Such testing is important and should be applauded: it sheds light on the financial stability of such arrangements and improves our knowledge of ways of ensuring consumer protection. I look forward with considerable interest to the outcomes of these pioneering ventures.

Nicholas Barr
Professor of Public Economics, European
Institute, London School of Economics

Acknowledgments

I wish to thank the people and the institutions that made this book possible and, in particular, Patricia H. Werhane, Ruffin Professor of Business Ethics at the Darden Graduate School of Business Administration. Professor Werhane guided me in the writing of this book from the first to the last chapter. Her expertise in ethics and philosophy was important for the development of a financial instrument that has deep ethical consequences, and her comments reflected that. She guided me through the steps required to complete this book, and her support allowed me to pursue the topic fully. I am grateful to have had the opportunity to work with her.

I am likewise indebted to Robert F. Bruner, Distinguished Professor of Business Administration at the University of Virginia and Executive Director of the Batten Institute. The inspiration for developing this idea into a book started in Professor Bruner's office, and he has thereafter been committed to my full exploration of human capital contracts (HCCs) and their implications. His help came in various ways: he offered many ideas and suggestions on the topic, guided me on a preliminary project, of which chapter 10 is a result, and read several versions of many chapters in addition to a complete draft of the manuscript. However, I am most grateful for his continued enthusiasm for my continued research in the area.

I am also indebted to the Batten Institute for underwriting my full-time exploration of HCCs, at both an academic and an entrepreneurial level. Elizabeth Faulkner O'Halloran, the Institute's Director of Intellectual Capital, ensured the successful completion of this work. She provided continued support from the Institute, expanded the scope of the original projects to include a conference and ancillary research projects on the topic, commented on the manuscript, and managed the production of the final product. I am most grateful for her responsiveness at critical moments during which I needed support to continue writing. Amy Halliday edited and commented on several chapters.

Steve Mendenhall also read an early manuscript. Finally, I always received the help I needed from Debbie Fisher and Donna Gowen. Thanks to their support I could fully concentrate on writing this book.

Camilo Soza was the first contributor to the ideas in this book. We were inspired by the emission of the Bowie bonds, the instrument through which the singer David Bowie sold part of his rights to proceeds from future concerts and royalties. That discussion was the seed from which my interest on this topic grew.

My father, Hugo Palacios Mejía, aided me during the beginning of my research. Many of the ideas brought forward in this book were originally conceived in conversations with him. Thereafter, he continued to offer his comments and advice, something he has done with my mother, Maria Mercedes Lleras, throughout my life.

Harry Patrinos of the World Bank and Jack Maas of International Finance Corporation (IFC) reacted initially very positively to my interests and made several suggestions on how to develop them. It was through them that I was able to contact several academics and practitioners currently involved in the design an implementation of innovative instruments for financing higher education.

Professor Nicholas Barr, Professor of Public Economics at the London School of Economics and Political Science, reacted enthusiastically to the possibilities of combining human capital contracts with income-contingent loans. I am thankful for the kind words and incisive analysis presented in the foreword for this book. Professor Bruce Chapman, Director of the Centre for Economic Policy Research at the Australian National University, was also very interested in the ideas presented here. He shared his extensive knowledge on the implementation of income-contingent loans and commented on an earlier draft. Their comments improved the quality of the original draft's content significantly.

Professor D. Bruce Johnstone, University Professor of Higher and Comparative Education, at the Department of Educational Leadership and Policy of the University of New York at Buffalo, provided further information related to income-contingent loans. Professor Johnstone discussed with me his views of income-contingent loans and his reactions to HCCs. Mort Engstrom, Director of Capital Management at Yale University provided information concerning Yale's Tuition Postponement Program (TPP) and participated in a workshop organized by the Batten Institute.

Roy Chapman, CEO of Human Capital Resources, Inc., made substantial progress during the 1990s on the implementation of human capital contracts and it was encouraging to see how close he was to actually implementing them. Although he is quoted directly in only a few segments of this book, his ideas are spread throughout it. Without the information that he provided, as well as our several conversations, this book would miss an important point of view. It is my wish that its publication aids him in the implementation of this kind of contract.

Vishal Garg and Raza Kahn, co-founders of Iempower, Inc., were the first to offer HCCs in the USA. They provided many insights on how to implements these contracts and on what their future development might be. I admire their courage in starting with this innovative product and hope that they can capture value from the path they are opening, a path that can transform higher Education financing. The existence of their company increased my confidence on the applicability of HCCs and was an inspiration for completing this work.

Felipe Vergara led the creation of Lumni LLC, a company that structures funding for students through HCCs. This experience has provided important insights into the challenges of implementing these contracts in developing countries, the perceptions of investors, and the possible solutions available to reduce the risk involved in this investment. Lumni received help from Gonzalo Labbe, and legal advice from Felipe Bahamóndez, Rafael Bilbao, Alvaro Cuevas, Gustavo Cuevas, Andrés Fernández and Alvaro Ramírez. Patricio Tapia's faith in the project, as well as his interest and support, led to the first HCC fund in Chile. I wish to thank Jorge Andueza, Patricio Canto, Claudio Elgueta, Ernesto Ezquerra, Gonzalo Soffia, and Patricio Tapia for their participation in the Andrés Bello Uno Fund.

The following people provided insights – perhaps without knowing it – that greatly enriched the book. In alphabetical order they are: Momina Aijuziddan, Alan Beckenstein, Grant Brown, Sherwood Frey, Luis Gallo, Tiha von Getzy, Les Grayson, Eric Howell, Hunt Howell, the late Juan Luis Londoño, Pedro Medina, Jairo Núñez, Hans Paris, George Psacharopoulos, María de los Angeles Santander, and Marta Juliana Silva.

Finally, I am profoundly grateful for the support of Jessica Chan, who played an important dual role throughout the development of this book. In addition to devoting countless hours to discussing these ideas with me, and many others to reading and editing the manuscript, she provided the emotional sustenance that made dedicating myself to writing an easy task.

I am grateful for all the help and all the contributions made in different ways by the people mentioned above. The errors and limitations of the book, of course, remain my own.

MIGUEL PALACIOS LLERAS

Introduction

I MAGINE that a student who wants to attend college, but does not have the resources to do so, signs a contract with an investor in which he commits to pay 10 percent of his income for twenty years after graduation in exchange for $100,000 received today to pay for tuition fees and living expenses. This contract, which gives the investor a 10 percent stake in twenty years of the student's income, is an equity-like instrument named here a "human capital contract (HCC)." This book provides an answer to why exploring these instruments matters, why their existence is desirable, how they can be implemented, how they relate to other instruments available for financing higher education, and the implications of all this for designing instruments for financing higher education.

Private funding of higher education

The first important point to consider is that greater participation from private markets is required to face the increased demand for attaining higher education throughout the world. The participation of private sources in the financing of education can increase capacity in two ways. First, private sources offer students a mechanism for financing their education – the whole idea behind this book. And second, where institutional arrangements permit, private markets will direct resources with some regard for the quality of education offered by different universities, thus creating pressure on higher education administrations to be more competitive.

But private capital will come in only if the prospect of obtaining a positive return, *vis-à-vis* the risk taken is attractive to investors. Depending on the characteristics of the investment, different mechanisms can be used to attract capital. The two main categories are debt and equity. The appropriate combination of these two depends on the particular risk profile of the project.

1

Equity is used for investments with high-risk profiles where the use of loans would be excessively costly, if not impossible. The use of equity suits risky investments better because investors compensate possible loss through a significant financial upside potential, well above the original value of the investment. With debt, all investors have is downside. The main argument of this book is that debt is not the best mechanism for financing education, and a different approach, one that considers equity investments, should be explored.

To explore these instruments, the book's argument takes a different view from that which states that markets for human capital in a non-slave society cannot exist. I argue here that they can exist if the market trades are based on the earnings of individuals, not on the activities they will perform. This view is very important, as the absence of a market for human capital in a free society is brought forward as one of the reasons why capital is not attracted to education investments, in spite of their relatively high rates of return.

The time is right to explore such instruments. Financial markets have been transformed since the 1980s, enabling the combination of assets in ways that were not possible before. Two changes are particularly relevant: the rise of investment funds and the securitization of assets. Thanks to these advances, a market for instruments whose value is driven by human capital is conceivable. Such a market would offer more choices to students, make information on the value of education more transparent, and facilitate the implementation of education financing schemes.

The road ahead

This book consists of three parts. Part I lays out the context of human capital, why it is relevant, and why traditional methods fail. Further, it points out why the only plausible direction for seeking alternatives lies in the private sector. Part II describes HCCs in detail, starting from the history of the idea, and continuing through how they will operate and the reasons why they are desirable. This part concludes with the introduction of human capital options (HCOs) as a link between instruments based on the value of human capital and other forms of financing education. Part III analyzes issues related to the implementation of HCCs. It includes a description of the hurdles to implementing these contracts, lessons derived from the implementation of income-contingent loans (ICLs) and proposals to expand the use of HCCs in the light of institutional constraints that do not permit their implementation exclusively by the private sector.

Chapters 1–3 make up part I. Chapters 1 and 2 explore why, despite education being an excellent investment, there is not enough capital for financing it. Education has great benefits for the student as well as for society. The measured returns to investments in education reflect under-investment in this activity, resulting in costs for individuals and for society.

Chapter 2 proposes that under-investment in education is the result of a market failure. Education is a high-risk investment for the student and, because it lacks collateral, for the lender (if, indeed, there is one). High-risk investments are dealt with in financial markets through equity investments, which is not currently an available alternative for funding education.

Given the importance of education for a country's development, governments have addressed the problem by financing and operating educational institutions. This solution, however, is not sustainable in the light of the fiscal constraints faced by governments. Chapter 3 elaborates on this point in more detail. The high opportunity costs from under-investment in education in developing countries make the search for alternatives even more imperative.

Part II contains chapters 4–7. Chapter 4 presents the history of income-contingent repayment schemes, a proposal that addresses the market failures found in the traditional methods for financing education. The presentation starts with Milton Friedman's suggestion to use an equity-like approach to financing education, continues with ICLs, and shows how the natural development would be the development of HCCs. Chapter 5 describes how HCCs would operate in practice.

Chapter 6 makes the case for HCCs in detail. The case is based on the risk transfer that takes place between the student and the investor, and on the market incentives that HCCs create. For instance, the pricing of HCCs would favor universities with a proven track record of producing students whose earning power upon graduation is high relative to the costs they incur to attend that university, rather than universities with low education costs. Further, because high-income earners pay more than low-income earners, there is a redistribution implicit in the system. Thus, HCCs promote *equity* at the same time that they enhance *efficiency*, a characteristic that makes them an ideal policy to be sought by government.

Chapter 7 goes beyond HCCs and introduces HCOs as a financial instrument that can be used by students as an additional tool to manage risk. This chapter proves that HCOs can be used in combination with other financial instruments to design a wide variety of programs, such as income-contingent loans, to protect individuals against low-income situations.

Chapter 8 introduces part III of the book, explaining why HCCs are not widely used today. There are several hurdles. First, there are legal issues. Second, there are ethical concerns; some might compare HCCs to indentured servitude or partial slavery. In the economics of education theory, markets where future earnings are traded have traditionally been considered the same as markets where future human services are traded, making such markets incompatible with a non-slave society. I argue that in fact those views of human capital markets are not the same, and that the first is compatible with a free society while the second is not. Third, there are also financial concerns, such as the long-term nature of the cash flows and difficulty in the collection of payments.

Chapter 9 studies the implementation of two different programs of ICLs to offer insights into the implementation of HCCs and HCOs. The two cases presented are Australia's HECS program and Yale's Tuition Postponement Program (TPP). The chapter also makes reference to other ICL programs, such as those in Chile and Sweden.

Developing countries face additional hurdles in implementing HCCs. To address this reality, chapter 10 discusses two adaptations for the implementation of HCCs. The first seeks government collection of payments, as is done with ICLs in Australia. The second uses the same concept of equity financing, but targeted towards elementary education.

Chapter 11 wraps up the book by addressing the place of HCCs as part of a national strategy for massive higher-education financing. It closes by exploring some possible consequences of implementing HCCs throughout the world.

A more technical approach to the valuation of HCCs and HCOs can be found in the appendixes. Appendix 1 presents a framework for the valuation of HCCs that predicts how investors would price these instruments. The appendix includes a solution using the results derived from human capital theory, particularly from Gary Becker's and Jacob Mincer's work. The resulting equations permit an analysis of the role that different variables play in the valuation of HCCs. Appendix 2 analyzes the valuation of HCOs, and shows how different types of ICLs can be valued using HCOs. Appendix 3 contains tables that compare the attributes of HCCs and ICLs. As a numerical example, appendix 4 develops a hypothetical case using data on the returns of education in Colombia. The example will be used to illustrate how parameters in HCCs can be designed such that they become financially successful. This example should serve as a guide for policymakers interested in determining reasonable estimates to implement the contracts.

I | *The problem of financing education*

1 | *The value of education*

T HIS book addresses a way of financing education based on its economic value, through an arrangement defined as a human capital contract (HCC). The term "human capital contract" derives from human capital theory, the modern economic theory that recognizes the knowledge and skills of an individual as a form of capital. Hereafter, "human capital contracts" will be referred to as HCCs.

HCCs are based on the assumption that education has economic value. The value of education, though, is much wider than merely economic. For the discussion that follows, I will discuss the moral and economic value of education. This separation is convenient because moral arguments offer compelling reasons beyond the purely economic ones for investing in education. It is important to keep in mind, though, that the moral justifications alone are not enough to produce economically viable alternatives for financing education.

At least three *moral* arguments call for investments in education. First, education permits a person to make better use of her intelligence, it being the single human attribute that allows human beings to transform things found in nature into things that are useful for other human beings. By aiding intelligence, education raises the potential of human beings to transform reality for the benefit of all.

The responsibility for the benefits that humanity receives as knowledge advances falls on educated individuals. When Newton states that he was standing on giants' shoulders, he was acknowledging that he was only furthering the path that others had opened up for him. He would have not been able to do what he did had he not been exposed to the works of those giants. The solution of problems that lie on the frontier between knowledge and ignorance rests mainly on the shoulders of those who have been educated. Their education walks them to the frontier of knowledge in a few years along a path that took humanity thousands of years to build. Unless aided by luck or exceptional wit, those who have walked the path of knowledge are the only ones who can continue building on it. This reason compels Marshall to state that "All that is spent during many years in opening the means of higher education to the masses would be well paid for if it called out one more Newton or Darwin, Shakespeare or Beethoven" (Marshall, 1956/1890, bk. 4, chs. 6, 7).

Second, educated people can also do things for themselves, since they can use their knowledge to improve their quality of life. In a modern economy, the use of intellectual capacity and knowledge is rewarded with higher salaries. This may well be the only real alternative for individuals who are born into low-income families. The moral value of education stems from the additional choices it offers to individuals, including the possibility of a more comfortable lifestyle.

Third, education is also commonly cited as a source of stability in modern democracies. Stability comes from being able to transfer a set of commonly accepted values that can hold social institutions together without the use of coercion. Jefferson's quote at the beginning of this volume refers to this very point which, if accepted, could well be the most important of all.

The values of advancing humanity's knowledge, of having a life beyond the minimum subsistence level, or of living in a stable democracy are qualitative and cannot be quantified; thus, the value of education that arises from these benefits cannot be quantified.[1]

However, in a world of scarce resources, education must compete with other investments whose value can be quantified for investors, both public and private. As such, the case for education has to be made on the basis of its economic value if it is to compete successfully with other investments. The arguments brought forward in this book for investing in education therefore rest on its economic value.

The economic value of education

The economic value of education comes from growth in productivity following training. The following subsections discuss who benefits from that value, how it is measured, and some estimates of its magnitude.

Education has economic value

The increased productivity brought about by education, particularly higher education, has been debated for a long time.[2] It is important to address this debate before moving forward with the assumption that education has economic value.

The hypothesis that denies economic value in education states that although additional education is related to higher income and productivity, education does not *cause* them. This hypothesis states, correctly, that confusing correlation with causation is analogous to stating that just because there is a relationship between weight and height, weight *causes* someone to be tall.

Proponents of this hypothesis argue that education aids employers in assessing the quality of a prospective employee, but that the productivity of the employee is given by ability and other factors independent of education. Highly capable individuals need a way of differentiating themselves from less capable ones. To do so, they obtain further education as a means of *signaling* their capabilities to potential employers. In other words, they use higher education as a screening device to give employers information they lack. This is known as the "screening hypothesis."

Accepting the screening hypothesis does not diminish the rationale for promoting access to education, since highly capable individuals from marginalized social groups still need a chance to acquire education in order to differentiate themselves. Regardless of the validity of the screening hypothesis, a person's earnings are strongly associated with years of education. If HCCs promote a person's efforts to become educated, then they can help one to harvest the private economic benefits of education.

The acceptance of the screening hypothesis has an impact on the perceived proper role of government in financing education. If education does not increase productivity, then the alleged socio-economic benefits of education do not exist, and there are no externalities, or "neighbor effects," from higher education. This implies that government should not subsidize the activity.

Although education can serve *in part* as a screening device, it is difficult to deny that education does have an impact on productivity. The fact that specialized knowledge is in many cases required for performing certain jobs implies that such knowledge has an impact on the performance of the worker. It is inconceivable to have an engineer learning "on the job" how to perform an appendectomy; it is much more efficient to have a medical doctor who has been educated as such in the operating room. At the very least, the diversified nature of the knowledge imparted in higher-education programs serves as a matching mechanism for employers looking for employees with a particular set of interests.

Thus the screening hypothesis does not completely disqualify the claim that there are productivity gains from education. Education *does* have economic value even though quantifying its real value is increased by the difficulty of measuring the "screening" effect.

Private and social value

The value of education can be examined from two different points of view defined by who captures or benefits from it. The first point of view is the individual's, the second, society's. When analyzing the value of education to the individual the subject of study is the *private* value of education. When analyzing the value of education for society, the subject of study is the *social* value of education.

The private, or individual, value of education can be divided in two parts: first, the satisfaction an individual derives from the mere fact of knowing and understanding the surrounding world and, second, the increased productivity an individual can achieve thanks to the additional knowledge and understanding acquired. This distinction implies that education has value in itself, as a consumption item, and in the fruits it will produce, as an investment. The consumption value of education is difficult to quantify. However, the value of education as an investment is relatively easy to determine: the private economic value of education comes from the additional earnings an individual can obtain with additional years of schooling. Most of the research studies that present a case for additional investments in education have focused on the value of education as an investment (for example, see Psacharopoulos, 1994). Even without including consumption value, the private value of education seems to be significant.

The social value of education is much more difficult to measure and exists only if the screening hypothesis mentioned in the previous subsection is not completely true, i.e. there is some productivity gain from education. In that case, more education translates into higher economic growth. For instance, new growth theory has given a renewed emphasis to the importance of education in the development of nations.

A country's growth is influenced by the education of its people because productivity is one of the main drivers of economic growth. Whether the use of technology is widespread or not depends on the capacity of individuals to make use of it. Without education, the use of technology in a country is delayed, and a delay in the introduction of technology is a delay in productivity, which translates into a delay in economic growth. Estimating the proportion of economic growth attributable to investment in education is extremely difficult, though some attempts have been made to provide a range of possible values. At the dawn of human capital theory, Nobel Prize winner Gary Becker (1993) cited Denison for his study on the impact of education on the growth of the United States growth from 1929 to 1957: "According to Denison, about 0.58 percentage points of the 1.60 percent average annual growth from 1929 to 1957 in national income per person employed are explained by the growth in knowledge, and about 0.67 by the growth in education."[3] If these numbers are accurate, the conclusion is that education accounts for *more than half* of the USA's growth during the period quoted. Observations that correlate education with economic growth have accepted the importance of education in the development of nations. Some studies place it as the most relevant factor; see for instance, Azariadis and Drazen (1990).[4] The debate is still alive today: Moretti (2002) uses earnings information and graduate population concentration to make an estimate.

Lester Thurow makes a strong argument in favor of investments in education as a source of competitive advantage for nations in the twenty-first century: "today knowledge and skills stand alone as the only source of comparative advantage."[5] Later he asserts: "Success or failure depends upon whether a country is making a successful transition to the man-made brainpower industries of the future."[6] There are reasons to believe that the impact of education on a country's performance will increase in the future.

The difference as to who benefits from the value of investing in education – individuals or society – has important policy implications, particularly with regard to who pays for the investment. This discussion will be resumed in chapter 3. In the meantime, it is important to establish only that there is more than one dimension to the economic benefits that result from investments in education.

Calculating value: net present value and returns

Scholars have been attempting to measure the value of education for at least the last forty years, proposing a model for explaining the

Table 1.1 *Fees as a percentage of student private expenditure, 1995*

Country	Fees as a percentage of total direct private expenditure	Fees as a percentage of total net private economic cost[a]
Ontario, Canada	22	14
Colombia, public	4	2
Colombia, private	19	14
India	18	11
USA	25	15
China	9	Na
Kenya, public	11	7
Kenya, private	42	30
Indonesia, public	10	Na
Indonesia, private	20	Na

Note:
[a] Includes forgone earnings.
Source: Ziderman and Albrecht (1995, 38).

relationship between education and income. Becker (1993) proposed formally that education had initial costs, like any investment, and that it had offsetting economic benefits over the productive life of the individual. The value of education is thus the present value of the difference between the benefits of education and its costs.

Measuring private and social value

The economic value of education can ultimately be measured in dollars (or the local currency). In doing so, all cash flows affected by the investment should be included in the calculation. The most important are (1) forgone earnings, (2) expenses for tuition, books and other supplies, (3) additional expenses such as room and board, and (4) the incremental income gained from the additional education. The first three items are the costs of the investment, while the last one represents the pay-off. The relative weight of tuition, usually believed as the most important cost for the student, is shown in table 1.1.[7]

Measuring the private value of education requires including as part of its costs only the expenses for which the student actually pays. Adjustments are made for additional resources students receive from government. As a consequence, measurements of the private value of education will necessarily include decisions made by government.

On the other hand, an estimate of the social value of education includes all the costs and benefits used in the calculation of private value *and* all the costs and benefits that the individual does not incur or enjoy. All the private benefits and costs should be included because these have social value. An individual's income represents at least part of the value that society derives from her work, while the costs privately incurred by the individual makes use of society's valuable scarce resources. Calculations of social value that take into account only the costs for which the individual does not pay and the benefits for which she is not compensated ignore this. Calculations of social value that ignore the costs privately incurred and the benefits privately earned should be used only to measure the impact of investing in education on the state's finances.[8]

Thus, to estimate the social value of education, two adjustments need to be made to the estimation of the private value: first, the full cost of education is considered, regardless of who pays for it; and, second, the additional income that society derives from the student's productivity that is not reflected in the student's own increase in income must also be reflected. The adjustments have opposite impacts on the estimated value of education. This means that the social value of education can either be higher or lower than the private value, depending on the relative value of the costs not paid and benefits not captured by the individual.

The common assumption is that the extra income that individuals cannot capture is much higher than the costs for which they do not pay. If this assumption is true, then the social value of education is more likely to be higher than its private value. For instance, Becker (1993) ventures a range between 12 percent and 25 percent (and states that that range is a measure of our ignorance on the social returns to education). However, because there has not been a satisfactory measurement of the income that the individual does not capture, most studies that have attempted to measure the social value of education have adjusted only the costs and have not made any adjustment to income. These studies *systematically under-estimate* the social value of education and will always show lower social values than private ones. However, the reader should always keep in mind that this is the result of a difficulty in measurement rather than a true reflection of reality. Social value measured without the benefits of the externalities produced by the individual can be useful only for setting the lower limit of the social value of education.

Value versus returns

In spite of the fact that the value of education can be measured in currency terms, human capital theory has traditionally used a different measure for valuing the economic benefits of education. Rather than obtaining a net present value (NPV) using an appropriate discount rate, economists have focused on finding the discount rate at which investments in education would yield a NPV of zero. The interest rate at which a discounted cash flow equals zero is defined as the internal rate of return, usually simply known as "rate of return." In common jargon, to measure the returns of education means to find the internal rate of return (IRR) on an investment in education. For simplifying reasons, this rate has been assumed to be constant for each additional year of education, although some distinctions have been made between elementary, middle, and higher education.

Investment decisions should be made based on cash flows discounted at an appropriate discount rate. However, using the IRR to analyze investments in education has at least two important advantages. First, the comparison of the IRR obtained from education with the rates of return obtained on investments of similar risk simultaneously answers two questions: (a) if the rate of return on education is higher than the rates of return on similar-risk investments, then the NPV of investing in education will be positive; and (b) the difference in the rates of return gives an idea of the robustness of the conclusion: that the NPV of the investment is positive. Second, the use of IRRs permits a comparison between countries where absolute differences might be misleading. For example, two countries could have the same value, measured in dollars, but one of them required a much higher investment. A NPV analysis would say that both investments are equally attractive. However, looking at the rates of return would show that one required a smaller investment. To make use of the voluminous information available on investments in education, the economic value of education is frequently discussed in this book as "returns to education."

Measuring returns: methodology

Scholars use two methods for estimating returns on education. The first, also known as the direct or comprehensive method, uses information on earnings and costs to estimate the rate of return. The second method, also known as indirect or Mincerian, uses only information on educational attainment and income.[9]

The direct method for measuring returns on education is more reliable, but also more complicated to implement. It is reliable because the parameters that affect the value of the returns are measured directly. However, measurement of all the parameters may be expensive and cumbersome; as such, the method is not always easy to implement.

The indirect method estimates the return to education from a cross-sectional regression of income against years of schooling. It is not nearly as reliable but is much easier to implement. It is unreliable because certain assumptions have to be made about the costs of education in order to obtain the desired results. These assumptions are true only in special cases and most of the time will only be approximately right. However, as shown by Mincer (1974), the assumptions made about the costs of education permit the researcher to estimate the return on education by measuring *only* the income differentials for different levels of educational attainment. The ease with which the rates can be estimated has made this method very popular. However, whenever possible, using the direct method for estimating the returns on education is preferable.

The size of the returns to investments in education

The returns to investments in education have been measured extensively in most countries of the world. The most comprehensive collection can be found in Psacharopoulos (1994).[10] Psacharopoulos has compared returns to investments in education for almost three decades, compiling results from many different countries, and conducting several studies himself. His 1994 global update is the third, confirming many of the original conclusions of his earlier papers. His compilation also has the advantage of including estimates on both private and social returns to education, a relevant distinction for producing policy recommendations. Table 1.2 shows both the social and private average rate of return for selected regions by level of education.[11]

To evaluate the attractiveness of investing in education from a private perspective, the private rates of return to education must be compared to the private rates of return obtained from investments with similar risk and liquidity characteristics. A frequent comparison comes from the returns obtained from investments in small manufacturing enterprises. These share with education highly risky results once the

Table 1.2 *Returns to investments in education, by* per capita *income group, 1994.*[a]

Region	Mean Per capita ($US)	Social[b] Primary %	Secondary %	Higher %	Private Primary %	Secondary %	Higher %
Low income ($610 or less)	299	23.4	15.2	10.6	35.2	19.3	23.5
Lower middle-income (to $2,449)	1,402	18.2	13.4	11.4	29.9	18.7	18.9
Upper middle-income (to $7,619)	4,184	14.3	10.6	9.5	21.3	12.7	14.8
High income ($7,620)	13,100	n.a.	10.3	8.2	n.a.	12.8	7.7
	13,100	n.a.	10.3	8.2	n.a.	12.8	7.7
World	2,020	20.0	13.5	10.7	30.7	17.7	19.0

Note:
[a] (Psacharopoulos, 1328). Table 1.2 shows the latest information available using the full method.
[b] Notice that social returns are always lower than private returns. As discussed on p. 14, this is the result of adjusting only the costs of education without including the possible benefits that the individual does not appropriate.
Source: Psacharopoulos (1994).

entire investment has been made, as well as the highly illiquid nature of the investment. Based on these considerations, the appropriate benchmark rate of return suggested by Psacharopoulos for education is 8.7 percent.[12] However Becker (1993) points out that the expected return should be somewhat higher to compensate for the fact that investments in education cannot be sold.[13]

The positive spread between the expected return on education and the required rate of return on investments of similar risk implies that there are opportunities to profit by investing in education. For a policymaker, the implication is that there is under-investment in education and that individuals are not making the most efficient use of resources. Further, if the assumption is true that the public benefits that the individual does not capture are higher than the costs for which the individual does not pay, then society as a whole is missing out on valuable investment opportunities.

The optimal amount of investment in education will be attained when the returns on investments in education equal the returns on other kinds of investments with similar characteristics. Education, like any other investment, has decreasing marginal returns: as investments in education increase, the expected returns decrease. As the returns from investing in education approach the returns obtained from other investments of similar risk, there will be no economic advantage from pursuing investments in education. At that moment, the marginal benefit from investments in education will equal its marginal cost (basically the opportunity cost not obtained from investments of similar risk). In other words, only when investments in education return around 9 percent can it be said that there is no under-investment in education. For now, as table 1.2 shows, a significant difference exists.

Under-investment implies that there is an opportunity cost for society and individuals. The existence of this cost is particularly pervasive because of its cumulative nature. A frequent quote in human capital theory comes from Alfred Marshall, who in the nineteenth century described this cost by referring to the children of the working class:

they go to the grave carrying with them undeveloped abilities and faculties; which if they could have borne full fruit would have added to the material wealth of the country – to say nothing of higher considerations – many times as much as would have covered the expense of providing adequate opportunities for their development.

But the point on which we have specially to insist now is that the evil is cumulative. The worse fed are the children of one generation, the less will they earn when they grow up, and the less will be their power of providing adequately for the material wants of their children; and so on to the following generations.[14]

The magnitude of the cost to society of under-investment in education is even more dramatic when one considers that the social returns to investments in education shown in table 1.2 do not reflect any of the externalities these investments produce. Social returns, without any of the external benefits attributed to education, are in themselves already higher than the rates of return obtained from other investments. Thus, the case for investing in education from a social perspective is very strong.

Table 1.2 also reveals information related to *where* the opportunities are higher for investing in education. The observed returns vary inversely with the income *per capita* of countries. This reflects the decreasing returns to which investments in education, as with any other investment, are subject. High-income countries have traditionally had much higher investments in education than lower-income ones. Thus, whereas in high-income countries returns to education roughly equal the returns of other traditional investments, low-income countries, particularly the ones in the poorest group, have a huge investment opportunity in education . A logical conclusion is that additional investments in education are most needed in low-income countries. This is the reason why this book is concerned with alternatives for implementing HCCs in developing countries.[15]

Along with information on where the opportunities are greatest, table 1.2 offers information about *when* the opportunities are higher for investing in education. Social returns are highest for elementary levels, decrease for secondary, and are least for higher education. This is another manifestation of the law of diminishing returns: each additional year of education produces lower returns. The conclusion is that efforts to increase investments in education will return higher values for society if concentrated on elementary education first and then on secondary education. Regardless of this observation, investments in *any of the traditional levels of education,* according to the data in table 1.2, will yield positive results.

Conclusion

This chapter has argued that education is valuable, and that society has under-invested in education. Therefore it is likely to "pay" for students, investors and governments to increase their investment. How this may be done is the central topic of this book.

HCCs empower individuals to obtain the resources necessary to acquire any kind of knowledge that produces economic value for society. Thus, HCCs can be used for either the formal, traditional ways of imparting knowledge, such as schooling at all its levels, or for life-long training programs. The high returns to investments in education that are obtained in different places of the world at least support the use of HCCs for formal schooling.

Although in theory HCCs can be used for financing *any* level of education and would be most profitable for elementary and secondary education, their implementation is not equally easy for all levels. In particular, investing in elementary education has at least two problems: first, since students in elementary education are minors, the implementation of HCCs requires a legal framework that allows a parent or guardian to engage with investors on behalf of the student; second, the long-term nature of the expected cash flows can make investors reluctant to invest. Thus, implementation of HCCs at the higher-education level is more feasible. Once HCCs have been implemented at this level, and their results tested, their usefulness for financing other levels of education will be seen more clearly.

The strong moral argument for investing in education is complemented by the economic value of doing so. Quantifiable results show that economically viable investments for individuals and for society are not being undertaken, with an opportunity cost for society. There are reasons why these profitable opportunities have not been financed, a topic that will be discussed in chapter 2. But opportunities exist and offer high rewards for those who seek alternatives for releasing the value lost by under-investment in education.

2 | Market failure in the financing of education

F ROM this chapter onwards the discussion will focus on higher and vocational education, also understood as non-compulsory and post-compulsory education (in contrast to compulsory education).[1] Because we are more familiar with the term "higher education," I shall use it throughout this book. However, the arguments I present apply to vocational training as well.

Higher-education students behave in fundamentally different ways from compulsory-age ones. There are two important differences that are particularly relevant. First, the goals of compulsory education are different from those of non-compulsory education. In the former, students are introduced to a set of fundamental common values to be required for them to live in society.[2] In the latter, students learn mainly for their own benefit. Second, school-age children, the direct consumers of compulsory education, are not capable of deciding how to obtain their education. In contrast, higher-education students are considered informed consumers making rational decisions regarding their fields of study (see Barr, 2001).[3] As a result of these differences, the potential for market failures in financing compulsory education are greater than in the financing of higher education.

Economic theory predicts that attractive opportunities for investment will disappear rapidly in the absence of structural barriers that prevent profit-seeking investors from taking those investment opportunities. Chapter 1 suggested that those structural barriers do exist in education. They are the reasons why there is under-investment in education, why students refrain from making the investment, and why investors shy away from financing it.

This chapter is devoted to illustrating those barriers. They can be divided into three groups: (1) those that influence the behavior of the individual; (2) those that influence the behavior of private investors; and (3) those that shape the environment in which individuals and investors make decisions.

Individuals

Investments in education are very risky from the point of view of the individual. To illustrate this point, Barr (2001, chapter 11) compares the decision to invest in education with a decision to buy a house, a low-risk investment for an individual.[4] Consider five points of comparison:

- **Unknown benefits:** Individuals know very well what they are taking on when they buy a house. All their lives they have (presumably) lived in a house and are thus acquainted with the needs that a house fulfills. In contrast, students hardly have first-hand experience of education. They do not know what they will learn and have not experienced the benefits of education. This is particularly true among prospective students from low-income families, since they probably do not even have a known example to serve as a role model in the pursuit of higher education. This group is likely to show little or no interest towards pursuing further education.[5]
- **Uncertain value:** Houses are unlikely to stop serving their purpose as long as they are not destroyed by calamities (hurricanes, earthquakes, etc.). Thus, a homebuyer knows that after making her investment it will not be necessary to make another one. Students, on the other hand, have no such certainty when they pursue further education. In particular, the probability of dropping out without completing a degree is relatively high and can greatly reduce the value of the investment.[6]
- **Need for constant reinvestment:** The value of a house will generally increase whereas the value of particular skills a student acquires through higher education can be rendered obsolete by technology or other better-suited individuals. In an extreme case, individuals may end up being unemployed, dramatically reducing the value of education to them. These threats are particularly potent in this age of rapid change and technological innovation. Individuals are forced to continually retrain and to engage in life-long learning activities. This would be equivalent to frequently relocating and refurbishing a house – a very costly activity.
- **Illiquid investment:** In the case of an individual financing a home purchase with a loan, the individual can sell the house or move into a less expensive one if mortgage payments become burdensome because of

decreases in income. In contrast, human capital cannot be sold because today there is no way of selling the future proceeds of human capital without enslaving the individual. In moments of financial distress, an individual cannot dispose of the present value of his investment in education; unlike a house, this investment is extremely illiquid.

- **Cannot be collateralized:** A house can serve as collateral for a loan, thus improving the terms a homebuyer can obtain on a loan such as through lower interest rates. Because the investment in education cannot be sold, it cannot serve as collateral. As a result, the terms that an "education buyer" can obtain on an education loan will reflect this additional risk in the form of less favorable conditions.

In the face of uncertainty a student who is risk averse is less likely to invest in education. Risk aversion can be expressed as the unwillingness of an individual to make a decision with a positive expected value.[7] In the case of education, risk aversion can be found particularly in low-income families, the very ones that cannot afford to pay for education on their own. As an example, consider a family with an average annual income of $US15,000; a debt of $45,000 represents three times their yearly income. This is an overwhelming amount, even more so when one considers that the family can hardly save anything from its yearly income, let alone take on an additional obligation. In these circumstances an individual might be hesitant to invest in education, even if the returns are likely to be positive. Thus, risk aversion mainly affects low-income families, the same group that has the least information regarding the benefits of education. As such, low-income families are the ones that will probably under-invest most in education.

An empirical graphical example can better illustrate the risks a student faces when evaluating the possibility of investing in education. Current information on the distribution of income by educational attainment is shown in figure 2.1 to illustrate how dramatic the uncertainty can be regarding the returns of an investment in education. The graph presents the distribution of income in the USA in 1999 of employed individuals between 25 and 34 years of age for two groups: (1) those individuals whose education was no higher than ninth grade, and (2) those individuals with a Master's degree. The information comes from the US Census Bureau, and includes data on more than 32 million Americans.

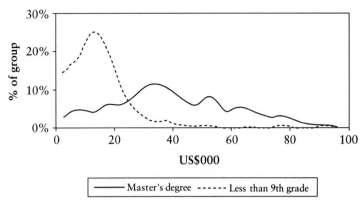

Note:
^a The graph is "smoothed" for easier interpretation by grouping incomes in $5,000 intervals and assuming an average income in the middle of the interval (for example, the average income of the interval between $10,000 and $15,000 is 12,500).
Source: US Census Bureau. Original table found in http://ferret.bls.census.gov/macro/032000/perinc/new03_021.htm. Data on incomes higher than $100,000 are not shown.

Figure 2.1 Income distribution for households in the USA, ages 25–34, 1999^a

The average income of individuals with an educational attainment of 9th grade or less was $16,252 while that of individuals with a Master's degree was $46,768. Medians were $12,770 and $39,305, respectively. On average, the difference in annual income was $30,516. This difference forms a compelling argument for investing in additional education.

However, the spread around the average shows a different story. While roughly 51 percent of the surveyed pool with educational attainment of less than 9th grade earned between $10,000 and $22,500 – approximately $6,000 around the average – 54 percent of individuals with a Master's degree earned between $27,500 and $62,500 – between $15,000 and $20,000 around the average. Thus, a student who plans to continue with a Master's degree will be much better off on average; however, how much better, especially after including education costs, is not that clear. In many cases, the student will actually be worse off.

This example shows that an investment in education can be very risky for the student. As a result, the amount that individuals will be willing to invest will be below the amount that they would invest if they could manage risk or add liquidity to the investment. This is precisely what is sought with the introduction of human capital contracts (HCCs), as will be discussed in chapter 6.

Lenders[8]

Possible private investors in education will also reduce the amount they are willing to offer, for the reasons discussed below. Following the above analogy of buying a house, financing education can be more difficult for several reasons:

• **Asymmetric information:** When financing homebuyers, lenders know very well what they are helping to finance because the value of a house is easy to determine. In the case of education, it is much harder for an investor to assess the value of the investment. The main complication comes from asymmetry of information. Students are the ones who best know their own capabilities, while lenders have very limited information. Missing information includes a student's ability, ambition, and intended career path. These factors compound with the sources of uncertainty that students themselves face, i.e. the value of their skills, unemployment, etc.

   Asymmetric information produces the well-known problem of adverse selection.[9] Under the circumstances described above, lenders will charge a premium (through a higher interest rate) for the capital they provide. This premium is designed to cover the uncertainty of the value of the investment that derives from what the investor does not know that the student *does* know about herself. The premium would deter at least some students who see in themselves high potential, ability, or drive. On the other hand, students with lower potential will be attracted to the offer they receive. The result is that the average student who would seek help from lenders will be of a lower quality than the average of the total pool of students. Lenders would have to adjust their premium to reflect the overall deterioration of the students who seek their help, deterring an even higher number of students. Eventually, the premium becomes so high that only the worst students apply for the investor's help. Students can take some actions to offer better information to lenders preventing the process from coming to this end. However, as long as there is asymmetry, lenders will be less willing to offer their capital at an average "market" rate.[10]

• **Difficult collection of payments:** When lenders help finance a house, the house will stay in its place and it will be relatively easy to gain control of it in case the owner refuses to continue payments for whatever reason. With investments in education, lenders can have a hard time locating the student, especially since more educated individuals have higher mobility. This gives rise to collection problems and to possibly high default rates that eventually make the investment less attractive.[11]

High mobility is an even greater problem for financing education in developing countries. Individuals who leave their countries are more likely to do so permanently since developed countries offer better opportunities and paychecks for highly educated individuals such as they may never find in their native countries. This contrasts with the scenario where an individual leaves a developed country, since in this case the move may be of a more temporary nature.

• **Uncertain value, illiquid investment, and absence of collateral:** The third, fourth, and fifth reasons are the mirror images of the concerns facing the student: third, there is low certainty regarding the value of the investment and therefore low certainty regarding the capacity to repay; fourth, in case the investment fails, individuals cannot sell their human capital; and fifth, because the investment cannot be used as collateral, the investor faces higher risk. In particular, students who most need financial help for their education are the ones who will have no other asset to offer as collateral to a lender.

Each of these reasons makes lenders increasingly wary of providing funds for education. Thus, the amount that they will be willing to provide for these kinds of investments will be lower than the amount that the average return on the investment could secure.

Other factors

Externalities

The existence of externalities will produce investment below the efficient social level. However, externalities do not by themselves explain why private investments in education are not undertaken despite the potentially high returns shown in table 1.2 (p. 18). We have seen that other reasons are also the cause for the lack of investment in education. Nonetheless, externalities should not be left aside when considering further investments in education, especially since individuals will have an incentive to invest only up to the point where the *private* return justifies it. Thus, even if all the problems with investing in education previously enumerated in this chapter were solved, there would be investment only to the level that satisfies private returns. There will still exist a market failure even if there are no frictions between borrowers and lenders. This market failure can be addressed only in a way that allows individuals to appropriate the benefits that society derives from their education. As discussed in chapter 1, however, the existence of this benefit is controversial (the "screening hypothesis"), and if it exists it cannot be determined precisely. There seems to be a consensus that the externality does exist, however, and that its existence requires the intervention of the state. How the state has intervened, and how it can intervene in the future, will be discussed in chapter 3.

Institutional issues

The idea that the state should oversee education has been in extreme cases taken to mean that the state should be the sole provider of education and that education should be free. Where this is the mindset, the role of private investors in education is considered suspicious, or outright intolerable. For-profit institutions are seen with some distrust, since decisions that affect students will be made on purely economic grounds.[12] Also, there is a fear that "greed" will decide who becomes financed, and how.[13] Therefore, in those places, the education sector finds itself a ward of the state and alien to profits or economic motivations.

As a result of this commonly held view, which in turn shapes institutions and their assigned role in education, investments in education follow political allocation processes, rather than economic or financial ones. And because education competes with many other functions that the state performs, it is unlikely that education will receive all the funds necessary to satisfy the demand for additional training. The results are budgetary constraints and the absence of private capital, which lead to under-investment.

This responsibility is burdensome in developing countries, where budgets are already insufficient for covering what is usually expected from them. Whereas developed countries can afford to have acceptable public education systems,[14] the result in developing countries is disastrous. This topic is discussed in more detail in chapter 3.

Conclusion

Investing in education, while churning out good returns "on average," turns out to be difficult owing to barriers that include mindsets, institutional arrangements, and incomplete information. The traditional solution, which relies heavily on government intervention, does not resolve these difficulties. The problems with the traditional solution will be explored in chapter 3. Regarding investment in education itself, understanding its complications is a first step toward offering ideas on how to overcome the obstacles such that everyone may have an opportunity to invest in it.

3 | *The need for alternatives to traditional funding*

S o far we have seen that there are opportunities for investing in education that generate attractive returns, and that those opportunities are hard to finance through the traditional lending methods. This chapter analyzes the ways in which higher education has been financed and why these solutions cannot cope with the increased demand that society will face in the future. Already, tuition fees have increased and there are growing worries on how to finance higher education costs.

Traditional funding

The traditional solution for funding higher education has been the direct financing and delivery by the state.[1] A basic model of state finance can be represented by figure 3.1.

Under this model, governments fund and manage higher-education institutions. Students receive free or nearly free education that in theory is available to all according to their academic merit. Many countries have followed this model. However, it has at least two problems: first, it can become inefficient; and, second, governments lack the resources to expand the system adequately.

A publicly financed and operated higher-education system can be inefficient because the consumers, i.e. students, cannot effectively influence the decisions of the public employees. The possibility of exerting this influence exists under the assumption that higher-education students behave like rational, well-informed consumers. Examples abound of poorly managed public institutions of higher education where the students' only option is not to attend. Thus, resources that could be used more effectively, either to better equip universities or attract better teachers (i.e. an increase in quality) or to increase the

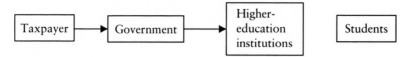

Figure 3.1 The pure state supply-side model

number of students that can be taken in (i.e. an increase in supply) are wasted.

One need look only at the fiscal crises faced by governments around the globe to conclude that, with perhaps a few exceptions, governments lack the resources adequately to expand the supply of higher education. Higher education competes not only with extremely important social investments, such as compulsory education and health, but also with public debt service, defense, and, in many places, corruption. Thus, expanding the supply of higher education using public funds is highly unlikely, if not impossible.

Private institutions of higher education provide a partial solution to the problem in those countries where such institutions are permitted. However, the high cost of offering higher education forces institutions to choose between providing an expensive service relative to the country's income *per capita* or offering a cheap but poor-quality service. Expensive institutions end up being attended by a small group of elite students, and cheap universities end up with the students that were not admitted to the better public institutions. In this case, also, supply is restricted not by the government's lack of resources, but by the population that can actually pay for the costs of attending an expensive university. The conclusion is that the sporadic creation of private universities will not solve the problem.

Alternative funding sources

Alternatives for increasing the supply of higher education without increasing the use of public funds must be explored. The potential solutions can be divided into two groups. In the first are those solutions that can increase the efficiency with which resources are managed. In the second are solutions that attempt to increase the amount of funds available. These are considered separately below.

Measures to increase efficiency

There are at least two ways to increase the efficiency with which resources are used in higher education: first, through better allocation
of government funds to public institutions, and second, through the
mechanism of competition. Ziderman and Albrecht (1995) have offered some suggestions that focus on the allocation process of government funds for increasing the capacity of public institutions. These are
not the central concern of this book. The measures that try to improve
efficiency through the mechanism of competition, on the other hand,
are relevant because human capital contracts (HCCs) are a means to
increase competition among universities.[2]

Permitting the existence of private institutions can increase competition by increasing students' choice. Where private institutions provide a
better quality of education than public ones, they serve as benchmarks
against which public institutions can measure themselves. Increasing
student choice, such as through the use of vouchers, allows students to
go to institutions where they can obtain the best value for their vouchers. Both measures increase pressure on public institutions to be more
efficient.

Public policy has already migrated toward schemes that increase
competition. Governments now recognize that they can support higher
education in two distinct ways: by financing universities and by financing students, and some are moving toward schemes where they finance
students rather than institutions. When governments finance students,
they receive a "voucher" that can be used to pay for education fees in an
institution.[3] With a "voucher" there is competition among all accred-
ited institutions to attract students. The voucher increases competition
because the effective price paid by students is reduced significantly, and
thus, students choose institutions based on criteria other than cost.

The shift is far from complete. Today governments finance higher
education by funding institutions and by financing students. The system
is a combined model illustrated in figure 3.2.

Although the combined model can increase competition, and thus
create pressure for a more efficient use of resources, the model is still
far from ideal. The idea that the whole cost of higher education should
come from government – i.e. the taxpayer and perhaps a small fraction
from the student – is, as explained in chapter 1, neither fair nor sustainable. It is not fair because it is regressive, as Psacharopoulos, Tan

Table 3.1 *Share of higher-education subsidies received by different income groups, 1986*

Country	Low-income	Middle-income	High income
Chile	15	24	61
Colombia	6	35	60
Indonesia	7	10	83
Malaysia	10	31	51

Note: The income groups are divided as follows (low, middle, high): Chile 30, 30, 40 percent; Colombia and Malaysia 40, 40, 20 percent; Indonesia 40, 30, 30 percent.
Source: Psacharopoulos, Tan and Jiménez (1986).

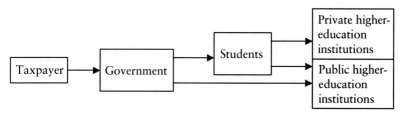

Figure 3.2 A combined "state-dominant" model

and Jiménez (1986) prove in table 3.1; it is not sustainable because of the fiscal pressures that governments face.

And even as competition increases, there is a limit to how efficiently higher education can be delivered using only public resources. After an "optimal" efficiency point is reached capacity may still not be enough to cope with the demand for higher education. This is especially true if countries improve their delivery of basic and secondary education, as many are doing, so a larger fraction of the new high-school graduates will want to continue on to higher education. For this reason we need to consider alternatives that increase the amount of capital available for financing education.

Measures to increase available resources

There are at least two ways to tap additional resources for education. The first is to solicit funds from other parties who may benefit from

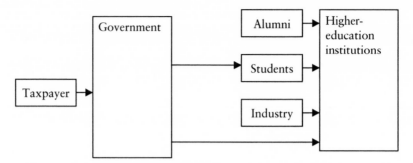

Figure 3.3 Income diversification strategy

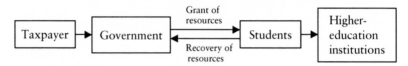

Figure 3.4 Cost-recovery strategy

knowledge and education. The second is to ask students to contribute resources themselves.

The first path – approaching third parties – is an *income diversification* strategy. This strategy recognizes that students are not the only "consumers" of the knowledge generated by the universities. By diversifying their income sources universities seek to utilize their assets, of which knowledge is the most important, in a way that serve other consumers besides students.

The main sources of revenue diversification are industry and alumni. Industry is willing to pay in exchange for knowledge that can be used profitably in the marketplace. Alumni, on the other hand, are willing to pay out of a feeling of gratitude or because they wish to use the contacts the institution has with industry. Figure 3.3 illustrates the cash flows using diversified sources of income. Income diversification strategies, however, are still not enough for covering the cost of teaching students.

The second way to increase available resources – asking the students to contribute – is also known as a *cost-recovery* strategy. The goal is to recover at least part of the cost incurred by the higher-education institution in providing education for students. In figure 3.4, the arrows that flow between government and students show the cost-recovery cash flows.

A cost-recovery strategy makes students pay for at least part of the cost of attending a higher-education institution. Chapter 1 addresses why this is a fair measure: students benefit economically from additional education and thus they should pay for at least part of this benefit. But a cost-recovery strategy can also damage access for students from certain social backgrounds if not implemented correctly.

Policymakers would thus seem to face the following dilemma: implement cost recovery to increase capacity and marginalize low-income students, or, do not expect students to pay back and restrict capacity. However, this dilemma is only apparent. Experience in the implementation of certain cost-recovery strategies has not damaged access.[4] The issues involved are explored below.

The student's perspective: cost-recovery without damaging access

The main challenge of implementing cost-recovery measures lies in how to avoid scaring away potential students from low-income backgrounds. This problem can be avoided if students know that they do not have to come up with financial resources while attending the university, and if they perceive that payments after graduation will not become unbearable. Let us consider whether traditional sources can satisfactorily address the student's funding needs.

Resources from government can be received through loans. Because of governments' own constraints, however, these resources cannot be grown fast enough to cope with demand for higher education. Private sources until now have worked only imperfectly for the reasons explained in chapter 2. Savings and wages (in the case of working students) can be considered only as a supplement for most students. In fact, working and studying at the same time can have negative implications for the performance of the student both at the university and at work, thus employment is not an ideal resource. Family and friends are the main source of funds for well-off students, but low-income students will not find a source of financial help in their families (figure 3.5).

Students from low-income families are therefore left only with government and private markets as their possible financing sources. But, as mentioned in chapter 2, students might be unwilling, for cultural and risk aversion reasons, to take on traditional loans from private markets. This leaves only the government as a funding source. But because

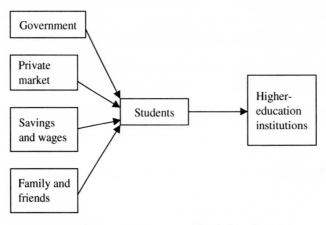

Figure 3.5 Students' main sources of funds for education

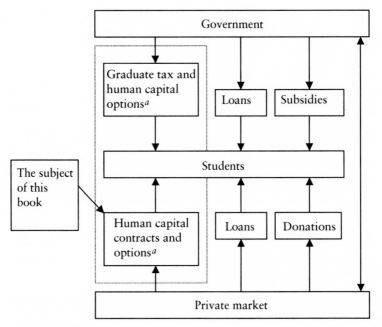

a Human capital options (HCOs) are an instrument derived from HCCs; they will be described in chapter 7.

Figure 3.6 Funding options for the student

governments have inadequate resources, private sources are needed to fill the gap.

Human capital contracts as an alternative

HCCs are a way for private markets to be more involved in financing higher education. These will be an additional funding option that, as will be explained in chapter 6, will complement other alternatives. HCCs provide a solution when other resources, such as family and personal savings have been exhausted. Figure 3.6 shows the funding options that students will have after the introduction of HCCs.

HCCs can take on an important role as *a major* funding source for students. They provide a way of expanding the supply of higher education, without marginalizing individuals from low-income backgrounds. The remaining part of this book is devoted to their study.

II | *Equity-like investments to finance education*

4 | *The evolution of human capital contracts*

I N chapters 1–3, I briefly explained why education is considered to be a good investment and why it is a key factor for economic development in almost every country in the world. I also briefly surveyed the traditional solutions that have been used for financing education and explained why those solutions are not the best ones. I will now discuss an alternative that addresses the main problems in financing education: human capital contracts (HCCs).

HCCs are contracts in which students commit part of their future income for a predetermined period of time in exchange for capital for financing education. I will use the following chapters to explain how this would operate and why HCCs should be considered a solution for financing education. This chapter will be devoted to tracing the origin and development of the idea.

Origins of the idea

The idea of committing part of one's future income in exchange for capital for financing education is not new. Milton Friedman mentioned the possibility of individuals selling a share of their future income in order to finance their education. Friedman first introduced the idea as a footnote in *Income from Independent Professional Practice* (Friedman and Kuznets, 1945), where he described the proposal as "an analogy that at first blush may seem fantastic." (Friedman and Kuznets, 1945, 90). In 1955, Friedman made a more detailed analysis in his paper "The Role of Government in Education" (Friedman, 1955). In its simplest form, Friedman's proposal was to create a financial instrument that would allow investors to "buy" part of a student's future income. He wrote:

The device adopted to meet the corresponding problem for other risky investments [not related to education] is equity investment plus limited liability on the part of the shareholders. The counterpart for education would be to "buy" a share in an individual's earning prospects. (Friedman, 1962, 103)

Friedman's work forms the basis of HCCs and his argument is outlined below.

When Friedman put forward his idea he was referring to vocational and professional schooling, as opposed to general education for citizenship. The reason why he focused only on vocational and professional schooling is because of the relatively small neighborhood effects of this stage of education as compared with general education for citizenship.[1] He argued that since the neighborhood effects are small, investing in vocational and professional schooling is a form of investment in human capital precisely analogous to investment in capital goods. This distinction framed the origin of HCCs for higher education.[2]

He then went on to note that empirical evidence suggested the existence of under-investment in human capital. This could be inferred from the differences in returns obtained by investing in human capital and investing in physical goods. The reasons for under-investment were explained in chapter 2, and boil down to the high-risk nature of investing in education. The counterpart for risky investments in financial markets is equity investments, where the investor takes on the extra risk because of the expectation of returns that will compensate for the risk.

Although it seemed to Friedman that there was no legal obstacle for contracts involving human capital,[3] he wondered why they did not exist.[4] He offered three possible financial explanations: (1) high administration costs, (2) the potential difficulty of getting accurate income statements, and (3) the long-term nature of the contract. He also mentioned psychological barriers, such as the novelty of the idea, the reluctance to think of investment in human beings as strictly comparable to investment in physical assets, and the resulting irrational public condemnation of such contracts. How his concerns would be seen in today's environment is analyzed in chapter 8.

Recognizing these difficulties, Friedman offered as an alternative investment by the state in the vocational and professional schooling of individuals. This would address most of the financial problems and seems to pose fewer psychological problems than if the investment were done by private financial institutions. However, the intervention of the state creates different problems, most important of which is the risk of turning the mechanism into a way of subsidizing vocational and professional schooling.

Despite the potential difficulties of implementing HCCs, Friedman emphasized the possible rewards from implementing them. Foremost among these was the potential of HCCs to create real equality of opportunity by enabling individuals from low-income backgrounds to access higher education. Other benefits in addition to this important one are explored in chapter 6.

The original idea becomes a loan

Friedman's idea immediately "ignited" the imagination of economists and policymakers and caused several proposals to be discussed at a national level, at least in the USA and the UK. Those proposals, however, shied away from the concept of "buying" a share in an individual's earnings prospects and turned instead towards lending with income-contingent repayment schemes (ICRS, see chapter 9). This may have been due to Friedman's very own words, since in the text immediately following the quote above, he refers to those who would "buy" a share in an individual's earnings prospects as "lenders," rather than as investors. The resulting instruments are now commonly known as income-contingent loans (ICLs).

Policymakers can design ICLs in different ways. The main variables are: (1) the income on which the estimate of contingent payments and the percentage paid is based, (2) the period over which the repayment would take place and/or the forgiveness conditions, if any, (3) the interest rate of the loan, (4) the collection method, and (5) the "buyout" features.

There are several ways of estimating the student's income that will be the basis for repayment of the ICL. In Friedman's original proposal, the income base should be the marginal income accruing from marginal education. Payment is made only on "new" income obtained from additional education. An easier alternative is to consider the student's entire income.

In theory, the repayment period of the debt would be the time it takes the student to repay the value of the loan. However, there will always be a percentage of students who will not be able to repay the entire loan and interest over their productive life. This raises two questions for the design of ICLs. First, what should be the maximum number of years that individuals should pay before being forgiven the unpaid portion of their debts? And, second, who should pay for the unpaid portion?

The answer to the first question is a matter of policy. Shorter periods of time will increase the number of students who do not complete their payments, while longer periods can create some political problems in the long term (see chapter 9). The answer to the second question has traditionally come in two ways: a third party subsidizes life-long low-income students, or high-income students subsidize low-income ones.[5] ICLs where a third party provides the subsidy for low earners are also called "externally subsidized ICLs." Those where high-income students subsidize the low-income ones are called "mutualized loans." Mutualized loans will be explained in more detail on p. 124.

The interest rate on the loan depends on what the lender wishes to obtain from lending the money. Not everybody will pay back at this interest rate. In an externally subsidized ICL, the subsidizing party, probably the state or an education institution, provides the subsidy. In a mutualized ICL, the *average* interest rate paid will be the one asked by the lender. However, some individuals will pay a higher effective interest rate to cover for those who pay less.

The collection method can have an important impact on the viability of the project. In his original proposal, Friedman introduced the idea that tax collection agencies could collect payments to reduce the administrative costs of student financing programs (as Australia and New Zealand do today). In contrast, other proposals had universities or banks collecting the payments (as Yale did in its Tuition Postponement Program, or TPP, see chapter 9). The collection method raised several political concerns and thus became a central issue in ICL proposals.

Finally, some mutualized loan programs provide "buyout" alternatives for high earners who wish to repay their obligations earlier. The "buyout" alternative places a limit on the maximum liability that a student will pay for the mutualized loan. The design of the buyout alternative is relevant to how the loan programs perform. The one implemented by Yale is especially relevant to this study.[6]

Income-contingent loan proposals

Some of the ICL proposals presented during the 1960s are described below to show how different economists proposed programs that varied in terms of the options described above. The following descriptions are based on Johnstone's account in his book *New Patterns for College Lending: Income-Contingent Loans* (1972).

The Vickrey plan, proposed by Columbia University economist William Vickrey in 1963, sought to rate students according to their ability to estimate their future income without education.[7] Payments would be based on the income differential between the individual's income after earning a degree and the average "expected" income without education estimated according to the individual's ability. The Vickrey plan estimated a "recovery" interest rate of 7 percent. The Shapiro plan, proposed the same year by University of Detroit economist Edward Shapiro, asked the same percentage of income from every student, regardless of the size of the debt, varying the repayment period up to a maximum of twenty years. The interest rate used in this plan was 4 percent.

The Killingsworth plan involved a proposal that resembled an equity investment more than a loan.[8] Under this proposal, also made in 1963, the student would pay a percentage of income *for a fixed period of time*, forty years. Of the fact that the repayment period was fixed, Johnstone comments: "the absence of a direct correlation between an individual's accumulated repayments and his total repayment obligation, plus the expectation that the plan will cover only a portion of the costs of money and administration, more nearly suggest an *income surtax* upon users of education than a loan."[9] The emphasis is his. As a "buyout" feature, the amount that an individual would pay in any given year would be capped.

A plan that caught more attention was the Zacharias plan.[10] The name came from Jerrold Zacharias, who chaired the President's Science Advisory Committee, the body responsible for making the recommendation in 1967. Under the Zacharias plan, students would pay through the Internal Revenue Service (IRS). Students who wanted to "buyout" their obligations would do so when their payments covered the loan at a predetermined "buyout interest rate."

A slight variation came in 1969 through the Rivlin report.[11] The report owed its name to Alice Rivlin, the Assistant Secretary for Planning and Evaluation at the Department of Health, Education, and Welfare. The proposal included several traditional mortgage-type loan repayments with forgiveness for low-income students. Each year a portion of payments would be forgiven for students whose income fell below a certain income level. The threshold income level would be determined each year. Thus, although students had low-income protection, the protection would vary somewhat arbitrarily each year.

Eventually, none of these proposals was implemented. However, the discussion did bear fruit and as a result, private initiatives were begun at the start of the 1970s. Yale's TPP is the most widely known among these initiatives. Less well known is the fact that Harvard and Duke started similar programs at the same time.

Loan or tax?

Given the important role that the state could play in the design of a nationwide system for financing higher-education, and given the possibility of using the taxing authority of the state, it was unsurprising that the idea of composing an additional tax for higher-education graduates was mooted. The Killingworth plan, which Johnstone suggested to be a "income surtax," was one such example. A similar discussion surfaced in the UK during the same period. Glennerster and Wilson (1968) discuss several proposals for using a "graduate tax" to finance higher-education. The concept of "taxing" higher-education graduates persisted in the literature of the time, and a "graduate tax" has been an option since then for the design of student repayment schemes.[12]

The definition of a graduate tax can be confusing. The word "graduate tax" has sometimes been used as a synonym for a government-collected ICL. For instance, Glennerster and Wilson (1968) suggest that payments could be for life, or until a given amount had been repaid. In the USA, Hartman (1972) called payments to ICLs "tax" payments. A "graduate" tax is understood in this book as a tax that all graduates have to pay for a specified period of time or for as long as the individual pays taxes. Therefore, Glennerster and Wilson's suggestion of taxing "until a given amount has been repaid," or Hartman's definition of "tax" as payments on ICLs, do not qualify as graduate taxes in this book. The "graduate tax" system has been discussed in the literature alongside ICLs (see for instance, Colclough, 1990), although to the author's knowledge it has not been implemented anywhere.

A "graduate tax" is in some respects closer to Friedman's original idea than an ICL. For instance, Friedman suggested that governments could collect payments from students, and given that these payments depended on income, they could be interpreted as a tax. However, unlike in a private initiative such as an HCC, the percentage of income that students would have to pay would depend on a political decision rather than on a market mechanism. Further, what creates most objections against the "graduate tax" is that it does not create financing alternatives for students, and does not reflect any correlation between what a student pays back and the cost of attending a higher-education institution.[13]

The first wave of income-contingent loan implementation

The discussions about ICLs eventually led to their implementation. Several private universities in the United States – Yale, Harvard, and Duke – stepped forward and created ICLs for their students. They were private initiatives in which these universities bore the risk of default by their alumni. No intervention from the state was required. However, probably because of increases in the availability of financial aid from the US government, these private initiatives were short-lived. Yale's ICL, called the Tuition Postponement Program (TPP), is described in detail in chapter 9.

What would have happened to ICLs in the USA had government not expanded its programs of financial aid during the 1970s is only speculation. ICLs might have become the common way of financing higher education. That speculation is moot, however; the reality is that ICLs did not become ubiquitous. Loans with lower interest rates, i.e. federally insured, became the main source of financing for students in the USA. ICLs became marginally important in the financing plans used by students.

The second wave of income-contingent loan implementation

The rich discussions during the 1960s and the early 1970s about ICLs faded away after the first attempts to implement them. There is a relative silence in the literature about these instruments after this time, with articles about the topic appearing only occasionally. The reason for this silence is not clear, given the advantages of ICLs over traditional "mortgage-type" loans.

Discussions about ICLs resurfaced, particularly after Barr (1987) revived the idea again in *The Economics of the Welfare State*. Shortly after that, the Wran report (1988) recommended the implementation of an ICL program in Australia. Thereafter Ghana, Sweden, Chile, New Zealand, and the UK adopted similar systems. At present, many articles about ICLs can again be found, and proposals for ICLs have been brought forward in a number of countries. Namibia, Ethiopia, and Hungary have considered implementing ICLs, or a graduate tax, to finance higher education for their students.

ICLs and graduate taxes eventually veered away from Friedman's original idea of using equity investments to finance higher education. Fortunately, financial developments in the 1980s and 1990s allowed a group of entrepreneurs to revisit Friedman's idea. These developments are the focus of the next section.

The new financial system

Financial systems, particularly in the major financial centers, underwent a spectacular transformation in the1980s and 1990s. Two important features of this transformation were the mushrooming of mutual funds of all kinds and the securitization of assets. These two developments, coupled with an increase in available capital, created a new opportunity for HCCs.

The existence of the mutual fund industry and the possibility of grouping assets together and selling them in parts changed the dynamics of how an HCC would work from the original idea proposed by Milton Friedman. In Friedman's original conception, the relationship would be between an investor and an individual. In the new financial order, the relationship would be between a vast group of fragmented investors (clustered into the mutual funds) and an enormous group of students (assembled through securitization).

This new arrangement protects both students and investors. Investors are protected because each individual student's performance will only marginally affect their return. In general, when investors invest in large groups, their return will vary more closely around the center than if the investment was in a small group. When students receive funds as part of a big group, they obtain cheaper financing because the investor bears less risk.

Returning to equity-like investments

Friedman's original idea developed into a new kind of debt instrument (ICLs) – one with low-income protection – but the possibility of developing an instrument that resembled equity did not die completely. After the financial revolution of the 1980s and 1990s an entrepreneur and a private initiative created a renewed interest in equity investments in human capital. The entrepreneur was Roy Chapman, who in the mid-1990s received public attention for re-launching the idea of "buying" a share in someone's income. The private initiative was Iempower, Inc. (operating under the brand name MyRichUncle[Ⓜ]), the first firm to actually implement Friedman's idea.

A new opportunity for human capital contracts

The renewed opportunity for the development and implementation of HCCs needed a "champion." In 1996, *Forbes* published an article on Roy Chapman, who attempted to push the idea forward again.[14] Chapman stated that he was interested in unlocking the value that inefficient education financing took away from society. For this purpose he founded and chaired Human Capital Resources, Inc.

The economist who originally thought of the idea, Milton Friedman, and Gary Becker, both Nobel Prize winners, endorsed Chapman's pursuit of this project.[15] They and other economists asked why the idea had still not gained momentum. Chapman believes the explanation lies in the absence of the legal framework needed to make it happen.

Chapman eventually refrained from creating HCCs – or Colsobs as he calls them – because of the legal uncertainties he faced.[16] (These uncertainties are described in more detail in chapter 8.) At the time of writing this book, Chapman is planning to go forward with his program if the US Congress legislates the legal changes he says are required for the implementation of HCCs.

In spite of Chapman's concerns, there is no unanimity on the impossibility of implementing HCCs under the current legal order. With less press coverage than Chapman enjoyed in 1996, MyRichUncle[Ⓜ] created and actually implemented HCCs in 2001. They are the first entrepreneurs to make Friedman's idea a reality.

MyRichUncle[Ⓜ]

Vishal Garg and Raza Khan are the entrepreneur founders of Iempower, Inc., the company behind MyRichUncle[Ⓜ]. They started working informally on investments in human capital in 1999, and eventually decided that they should work on them full time. Their interests are wider than the scope of this book, since for them financing higher education is only one of the many possibilities that investing in human capital offers. Financing higher education is, however, what they perceived to be the least risky investment with which to start. This is quite ironic, given that Chapman refrained from investing because of the risks (legal) involved.

Garg and Khan originally planned to launch their program in a few selected universities, using a very simple marketing plan: they distributed pamphlets in the campuses they selected. Aided by an unexpected appearance in the media, they faced a demand that greatly exceeded their expectations. Now they know that there is a significant market for their product in the USA, and plan to expand aggressively in the coming years.

The significance of Garg and Khan's achievement cannot be overstated. In launching this product they challenged the fears of others who have studied the proposal.[17] They are creating a new marketplace, one that gives new options to investors and students.

The way in which HCCs work is described in chapter 6. Suffice it to say for now that MyRichUncle[TM] offers financing with repayment periods of ten or fifteen years, permitting students to commit a maximum of 15 percent of their income, and asking from students a percentage of their income based on the university they are attending and the course they are pursuing.[18]

A global trend?

In their book *Future Wealth*,[19] Stan Davis and Christopher Meyer (2000) depict a future where human capital is recognized as the most valuable asset. The whole book rests on the assumption that markets will invest and trade in human capital.

Davis and Meyer observe how the trend is already well under way. It all started, they say, with the Pullman Group LLC's issuance of the Bowie bonds. The Pullman Group LLC, an investment bank, created a deal in 1997 through which David Bowie was able to obtain $55 million from the markets on expectations of future income from his concerts and royalties from the sales of his songs. The uniqueness of the Bowie bonds lies in the fact that the markets were willing to invest in an individual's capacity to generate future cash flows out of intangible assets: the rights to his songs and his income from performances. The

Pullman Group LLC has performed several similar operations thereafter.

These opportunities will be available initially only to talented individuals possessing extremely scarce skills: for instance, there is only one David Bowie. Other candidates are sport stars, artists, and in general, anyone whose name is of high value in the field where they perform.

However, the trend should eventually expand to skilled individuals in a wider variety of industries. Davis and Meyer cite the example of McKinsey alumni, as the firm calls their previous employees. The future of a McKinsey alumnus is likely to be good, thus markets should be willing to offer cash in exchange for a portion of the McKinsey alumnus' future income.

The recognition that human capital is a firm's most important asset should lead firms to invest in the human capital of their employees, even if they might leave the firm after completing their training. It might be better for a company to invest in part of the income their employees can generate and let them go wherever they choose, instead of attempting to retain them beyond the economically optimal point. In this way they do not lose the investment they make in their employees but still recover part of the value that those skills generate in the market.

Beyond companies investing in their employees, Davis and Meyer speculate on the idea of a résumé including an individual's fifty-two-week human capital "value" information. The implication is that every one of us with at least some level of skills will potentially be attractive to investors.

The use of HCCs to finance education is a natural extension of Davis and Meyer's thesis of the interaction that will exist between financial markets and individuals. If their predictions are right, then what seems like a novelty today will be part of our daily lives in the foreseeable future. The discussions then will center on new and more advanced ideas on increasing the returns offered by human capital.

The idea of using HCCs has advanced noticeably in the USA, similar advances have been made in other countries. Income-contingent programs, such as the one implemented in Australia in 1989 have been gaining popularity. However, those instruments are still loans. Most recently, the International Finance Corporation (IFC), the private investment arm of the World Bank, was interested in launching a program in Bangkok. The attempt failed, for two reasons. First, it coincided with the Asian financial crisis of 1997. Second, in the opinion of Roy Chapman, who was consulting for the IFC, Thailand lacked the necessary conditions for making HCCs work.

There are several reasons for why HCCs will be difficult to implement in developing countries. The main issues relate to the instability of the law, the difficulty in enforcing payments, the small size of financial markets, and the possibility of investors abusing students. All these factors make the investment less attractive from the point of view of the investor, and possibly dangerous for the student. I will expand on these problems in chapter 8. I will also offer two implementation alternatives that can permit the existence of HCCs in developing countries. These countries are the ones that need education the most, and the ones who should profit the most from the introduction of HCCs.

5 | *How human capital contracts work*

A s explained in chapter 4, human capital contracts (HCCs) are contracts in which an individual commits part of her future income for a specified period of time in exchange for capital for financing her education. This chapter discusses how these contracts would work.

HCCs require students to commit future earnings and yet, because the underlying philosophy is never to interfere with the student's free will, contracts should be signed only by individuals of legal maturity capable of making such choices for their future and future earnings. This condition excludes elementary and high-school students, since children are not recognized in most legal systems as valid parties to a contract. But creating financial alternatives for low-income students in their early years is of crucial significance. A possible alternative is discussed in chapter 10.

The description of how HCCs would work applies mostly to countries with developed financial markets. The basic features should be universal, in theory. However, countries with less developed financial markets will probably not witness the full development of HCCs as described in this chapter. Alternatives for implementing HCCs where local circumstances prevent their development based solely on private initiatives are discussed in chapter 10.

Basic features: the contract

The basic terms of an HCC specify what the student and the investor can expect from each other, the percentage of income that a student commits, and the amount of time that her obligation lasts.

The conditions that specify what students and investors can expect from each other are the most important features of the contract.[1] This is so because these conditions create a frame from which neither the investor or the student can depart.

The first and most important condition is "non-interference." Once the investor provides the funds for a student's education, the investor cannot influence or put pressure on the student in any way regarding her future behavior, particularly with respect to the job the student will take on once her education is complete. The importance of this condition cannot be over-stated. As long as students are absolutely independent, HCCs are a viable mechanism for financing education. If there is even a small possibility that the student is not independent, the contract can degenerate into indentured servitude. This condition of non-interference is reinforced by the creation of a market of securitized HCC funds. Even without this extra protection, the independence of the student should remain a basic principle of HCCs.

Some will argue that when investors offer different terms to students based on courses pursued or universities they take away independence from the student. The same argument is extended to the case of a student who switches courses, and is thus offered different terms by the investor for her remaining financing needs. Whereas the different terms that investors will offer to students in different courses and universities, or even their unwillingness to offer funding for certain courses or universities, will certainly influence the decisions that the student makes, the student has at any moment complete autonomy to decide what to do. For this reason, HCCs cannot be said to be a form of indentured servitude. (A more detailed discussion on this topic is presented in chapter 8.)

Second, the investor will expect from the student a certain percentage of her income as defined in the contract. For example, income can be based on the value in the individual's tax return statements. The investor will expect this payment during the specified number of years referred to in the contract *after* the student completes her education.

The investor will demand a percentage of income from the student based on the amount of capital provided as well as the risk of the investment. The investor may quote a percentage of income per dollar provided (or a multiple based on the amount provided, such as per $1,000 provided). The total percentage of income that the student commits is determined by multiplying the quote per dollar provided times the dollars received. For example, if an investor quotes 0.5 percent of income per $1,000, and a given student uses $20,000 dollars, the total percentage of income that the student will pay when she joins the workforce will be:

$$\$20,000/\$1,000*0.5\% = 10\%$$

The percentage of income committed will be cumulative. As a student advances in her studies, the percentage of income committed in previous years will be added to the percentage of income committed for the current year. For example, if a student commits 3 percent of income during the first year of college, and 4 percent during the second year, the total percentage of income committed by the student will equal 7 percent (3 + 4).

The percentage of income that a student commits for each dollar received does not have to be the same from one year to the next. In fact, as the time remaining to graduation comes nearer, the market should offer lower quotes per dollar because of declining risk and shorter time to the first payment. The specified period for which the student commits her income does not necessarily have to be the same, either. For example, freshmen might be asked to pay fifteen years after graduating, and seniors might be asked to pay only ten years after graduating. Although it might be cheaper from an administrative point of view to offer a "generic package," the obligation that the student takes on each year does not have to have the same terms as the one taken on in the previous year.

As an example, assume that John is going to enter a four-year program at a college where HCCs are available. After considering other financing sources such as family support, summer internships, and federal scholarships, he has the remaining financial needs shown in table 5.1. Total financial needs represent tuition, board, books and materials, and other living expenses. In this example, investors expect to receive a percentage of John's income during fifteen years. The percentage of income they are asking per $1,000 dollars provided for John's particular field of study and university is also shown in table 5.1.

If John decides to go ahead and finance the amount he needs through HCCs, he would commit 2.75 percent, 3 percent, 3.6 percent, and 2.8 percent in his first, second, third, and fourth year, respectively. At graduation, John would owe 12.15 percent of his income for the next fifteen years to the investors who provided the capital. If upon graduation John earns an annual salary of $25,000, he would owe $3,037 per year to the investors.

Table 5.1 *Example of human capital financing*

Year	1	2	3	4
Amount ($) (1)	5,000	6,000	8,000	7,000
% of income per $1,000 (2)	.55	.50	.45	.40
% of income committed ((1)/1000 * (2))	2.75	3	3.6	2.8
Accumulated committed % of income	2.75	5.75	9.35	12.15

Now contrast the cost of an HCC for John with a loan for the same amount. In this example, assuming that the interest accrued while studying was subsidized, John would have had to make a yearly payment of $3,037 on a fifteen-year loan for $25,000 if the interest rate was around 8 percent. However, as will be explained in chapter 6, John derives several advantages from engaging in HCCs, such as the fact that the amount he has to pay would decrease if his salary decreases, while the loan would remain fixed.

In theory, the design of a HCC is simple. But investors might add features to protect their investment and to make the contract more attractive to students. The following paragraphs discuss some features that are likely to be included when HCCs are created.

Additional features

Besides the basic parameters that determine an HCC, additional features can be incorporated to create incentives for students to enter into such contracts, and to ensure that students pay once they join the workforce. If these features are not included investors can obtain lower returns on their investment, and the viability of the HCCs could be threatened. The discussion below considers caps on payments, low-income forgiveness, caps on the percentage of income that students can commit, exit conditions, and variations in the repayment period.

Caps on total payments

In an HCC, when the student is very successful economically, the investor receives a sum much greater than the amount invested. Conversely, when the student is not economically successful the investor does not receive as high a return on the original investment. Thus, an alignment between the interests of the student and the investor occurs because the investor shares *all* the upside, as well as the downside, of the risk in the investment.

However, a problem that might arise with unlimited upside claim on a student's income is selection bias. Students who expect to earn very high-incomes *relative to their peers*[2] would not engage in HCCs because the cost for them would be more expensive relative to other alternatives. Thus, these students would seek financial support through different mechanisms, such as fixed loans. Conversely, students who think their income potential is lower relative to their peers would have an incentive to engage in HCCs, since that alternative would be much cheaper than others. The double effect of students with a perceived high-income potential migrating to other alternatives and students with a perceived low-income potential resorting to HCCs would distort the average profile of students who engage in HCCs. The resultant student pool engaging in HCCs would view itself as having lower overall income potential than would otherwise be the case.[3] This is the phenomenon of adverse selection.[4] If student's expectations are correlated with reality (possibly, but further research can illuminate this point), then adverse selection will result in lower returns for investors.

To prevent adverse selection, the percentage of income that investors require from each student should accurately reflect the future earnings potential of the student, including the possibility of a very successful economic future. If the percentage of income asked from students is perceived by them to be "fair" or acceptable relative to the value of their future earnings, students with both high and low earnings expectations will sign up for HCCs.[5]

Garg and Khan – the founders of MyRichUncle[TM] (see chapter 4) – claim that they can accurately price the contract for each individual. If their assumption is true, there should be no adverse selection because high-potential income and low-potential income individuals are priced differently, and each one gets charged a percentage that is proportional to their expected income. Garg and Khan go further and state that they have more information on what individuals will earn than those individuals do before earning a degree, thus contradicting the more intuitive notion that individuals know better what their earnings are going to be. In contrast, Roy Chapman (see chapter 4) believes that the investor will never know as well as the student what the student's

Table 5.2 *Expected present value of income: example*

	$
John	1,000,000
Mary	500,000
Peter	100,000

potential is.[6] This philosophical difference between the founders of MyRichUncle[TM] and the founder of Human Capital Resources, Inc. will affect the way in which they design their instruments. Only the proven success of either method will show which of the assumptions was correct.

Roy Chapman's view implies that HCCs cannot be priced accurately to prevent adverse selection. The use of a cap might be a way to address this problem. The cap would place a limit on the total amount that a student would pay while preserving the downside protection in cases of low income during the repayment period. Chapter 7 will discuss the interesting financial consequences of including a cap in an HCC. The following paragraphs analyze the effect on adverse selection of adding a cap to an HCC.

Consider three students: John, Mary, and Peter. Each of them will attend the same university and need the same amount of financing: $50,000. However, because each student will pursue different courses, the expected present value of income is not the same for each student. Table 5.2 shows what the estimated present value (using the investor's discount rate) of income for each student is for this example. Assuming Chapman's view is correct, investors do not know the difference in expected income and thus ask for a percentage of income from each student that returns a satisfactory return *on average*.

If investors are willing to finance the education of the three students with the expectation of receiving 10 percent of the student's incomes, the present value investors would obtain is:

$3* - \$50,000 + 10\% *(\$1,000,000 + \$500,000 + \$100,000)$

$= \$10,000$

Or 6.67¢ ($10,000/$150,000) per dollar invested

Under the assumption that students have a better idea of what their incomes will be, John may look for better financing alternatives. If he finds a cheaper means – one that implies a lower present value payment than $100,000 (10% * $1,000,000) – he would take it. The higher John assesses his future potential income to be, the higher the probability that he will look for a better alternative. If he does find a better alternative, he would not opt for the HCC, and the return that investors would obtain is:

$$2^* - \$50,000 + 10\%{}^*(\$500,000 + \$100,000) = -\$40,000$$

John's departure hurts investors. Their average income estimate turned out to be to high. But investors are not willing to lose money on their investments; thus they would change the percentage of income they required from students on the new contracts they offered, *increasing the amount that students would otherwise have to pay.* In this example, a new rate of 17.78 percent would produce a return of 6.67 cents per dollar invested:

$$2^* - \$50,000 + 17.78\% {}^* (\$500,000 + \$100,000) = \$6,667$$

However, as the percentage of income required by investors increases, the attractiveness of HCCs decrease, risking the financial viability of the entire system. As an alternative, suppose that investors place a cap on the payment amounts required from students. Assume that the cap is such that the present value of the payments a student will make during the life of the contract does not exceed $80,000 and that the percentage of income asked by investors keeps John in the system. The new percentage of income that will give investors a return 6.67 cents per dollar invested is 13.3 percent:

$$3^* - \$50,000 + 13.3\%{}^*(\$500,000 + \$100,000) + \$80,000^7$$
$$= \$10,000$$

Thus, in order to prevent John from leaving the system, the rate expected by investors changed from 10 percent to 13.3 percent of income. This difference does not relate to the returns to education, and thus distorts its measurement.[8] However, the feature prevents a much higher rate (17.78 percent) being charged and thus maintains the system's feasibility.

For students with the similar expected incomes, the cap should be proportional to the amount of capital that an individual uses for her education. For example, a student who commits 1 percent of income should have a lower cap than someone who commits 10 percent of income. If students have the same cap, there would be adverse selection among the students who need less capital since the cap would be high relative to their income. On the other hand, students who need more capital would have a relatively low cap. A proportional cap is defined by a maximum amount of dollars an individual will have to pay each year *per dollar invested*.

Low-income forgiveness

A second feature that can be incorporated into HCCs for the protection of investor returns is a lower proportionate payment for students who end up earning very low incomes. Low-income forgiveness increases the probability of obtaining any payment at all when individuals are in financial distress.

Another way of justifying low-income forgiveness is through the theory of the decreasing marginal utility of wealth. Given the case where two students have to pay the same proportion of their income, the one who earns less experiences a higher cost in terms of utility of wealth than does the one who earns more. At some moment this utility is so high that the individual becomes tempted to not pay at all. Like the caps on payments, the "forgiving" feature distorts the observed rate of returns on education, since the rate charged by investors would reflect this increased downside risk from the investor's point of view. Still, if the forgiveness feature did not exist, the risk that the investor would face could be higher, and the working of the whole system might benefit from the inclusion of additional financial protection for the student.

Maximum percentage of income committed

Investors need to consider the maximum percentage of income that they will ask from students. As the size of a student's total obligation under HCC increases, the relative cost for her of defaulting on the payments decreases. Thus, a student who has committed a large percentage of her income has an increased incentive to default on her payments. This will happen even when the absolute amount of income that the student gets to keep is enough for her to live comfortably. But this incentive will, of course, be much greater when the finances of the student are in distress.[9] A prudent financial institution limits the amount of capital it lends so as to avoid placing an individual in a situation in which her income is not enough to meet the repayment schedule.[10] A cap on the percentage of income a student commits would serve the same purpose.

There is also a moral argument against letting students commit a high percentage of their income in an HCC. Having a claim on a high percentage of the income of an individual, for example 60 percent or 70 percent, increases the power that the investor has over the individual, even when the individual is completely free to choose her occupation. Friedman is concerned with slavery when he writes:

There seems no legal obstacle to private contract of this kind, even though they are economically equivalent to the purchase of a share in an individual's earning capacity and thus to partial slavery. (Friedman, 1962, 103)

It is difficult to define the line where these contracts change from being liberating, enabling students to educate themselves and to fulfill their potential, to becoming oppressive. A general principle that can be used is that the contract is liberating as long as the total obligations of the student are similar, or lower, than those he would have had to pay with an alternate financing mechanism.

To avoid the moral problem the most prudent decision, both for the student and the investor, is to limit the percentage of income that a student can commit. From the point of view of the investor, this may mean forgoing a higher return on the investment. From the point of view of the student, this may increase the total cost of continuing with education. However, both benefit from the reduced risk involved in the contract.

Exit conditions

Nobody likes to enter into a contract from which they cannot exit if desired. HCCs can incorporate exit conditions for those who wish to terminate their obligations prematurely. The absence of such conditions can create an incentive in individuals to dishonor their obligations when they, for whatever reason, are dissatisfied with the contract.

Determining a cash amount that an individual has to pay in order to exit from an HCC provides a satisfactory exit condition. As with any other obligation, an immediate payment can solve the issue.

Notice that in essence, the exit condition is a call option on the unpaid balance of the contract.[11] Since students will exercise this option whenever the cost of paying for exiting is smaller than the value of payments to be made in connection with the contract, the exit condition turns an HCC into a capped one. The consequences of adding a fixed exit condition are the same as those described in the inclusion of caps and thus merit no additional discussion here.

Adjusting the repayment period

Under the basic contract, the repayment period is fixed. However, this feature may be inadequate for dealing with certain situations. One good example is when the student is deciding between working and pursuing additional education. A solution lies in defining the repayment period in terms of the time that the student has been employed. Under this variation, the basic contract would no longer oblige the student to pay for a fixed period of time, but for a fixed period of productive time.

For example, consider an HCC with a ten-productive-year repayment period. The student of this example graduated from the university and then worked for two complete years. Then, she decided to join a master's degree for another two years. Under the simple definition of an HCC, the student would still have to pay for six years after the end of her master's degree, while with the productive-year definition she would still have to pay for eight more years. By including the "productive" condition in the repayment period, the investor protected herself against the student's decision to join a master's degree.[12]

Similarly, since working part-time is also a choice for the student, one year of part-time work can be defined as half of a productive year. Therefore, if a student engages in a contract to work five productive years, and works only part-time, the obligation to pay would last a total of ten years.

The concept of "productive" periods solves many issues related to the decisions the student makes regarding her career. Under this definition, the risk for the investor diminishes considerably in situations like sabbatical years, work flexibility, additional education, and other similar situations. It also reinforces the idea that the investment in education, in which the investor is a part, has returns based on the productive efforts of the individual. This solution naturally reduces the incentive to invest in education with the view of not using it later.

With this feature we close the discussion on the possible variations that individual contracts can have to increase their attractiveness for investors. Possibly other variations will emerge as experience accumulates on student behavior. Now we turn towards the next natural steps that investors would take once they signed a contract with a student.

Beyond the individual contract: grouping students and investors

Recent innovations in financial markets may make it possible to raise capital to fund a large number of students by pooling contracts and issuing securities against these pools. This is desirable from the point of view of both the student and investor. The investor benefits from the diversification that pooling creates. Portfolio theory suggests that as long as the correlation between the incomes of students is less than one, the risk-adjusted return after diversification will be higher.[13] On the other hand, the student benefits because she falls into the anonymity of the group, decreasing the chance of abuse from investors. Also, since pooling a large number of students decreases the risk-adjusted return for the investor, the percentage of income asked by investors will presumably be lower.

Moreover, the grouping of students can spread administrative costs over a wide population of students, decreasing the administrative cost per student. Administrative costs would include collection, marketing and distribution, and research costs. Collection costs comprise all the costs related to keeping track of and invoicing individuals. Marketing and distribution costs are those incurred to attract students and to distribute funds to them. Finally, research costs are those that the fund will incur to determine which students to finance and under what contract conditions. Lower administrative costs increase returns to investors and reduce financing cost for students.

The amount of funds required to finance the education of a large number of individuals would bring groups of investors together in the creation of a fund. Such funds, which from now on I will call human capital funds (HCFs), will act as a bridge between large group of students and large group of investors. The nature of the fund is the

same one of mutual funds, where a group of investors invests in a group
of stocks. The possible combinations of students and investors in these
funds are infinite. In the following sections I describe my expectations
of how markets will react to these possibilities.

Groups of investors

Given that education is regarded as morally valuable independent of
its economic value, HCCs should attract investors who seek more than
pure economic returns. Since the main assumption of this book is that
education is a worthwhile economic investment, investors who seek
pure economic returns should also be interested in these instruments.
HCCs will also attract investors who measure value by other metrics.

Investors who only seek a market risk-adjusted return on their investment would treat an investment in a HCF as any other investment.
Such investors would make their decisions purely on economic terms
and would probably invest only in funds concentrating on economically viable careers and imposing very high standards on the students
they finance. These investors will seek under-valued opportunities and
invest in them. I will call them "economic value added" (EVA) investors. As I shall explain in chapter 8, they will be responsible for
unlocking large quantities of economic value.

Socially oriented investors will presumably also expect a return on
their investment. Unlike EVA investors, however, socially oriented investors will include in their measure of return the utility they get from
feeling that they are contributing to a worthy cause. The total returns
may be the same as that obtained by investors seeking pure economic
returns, but they will not measure it entirely in economic terms. I shall
call them Social Value Added (SVA) investors.

Alumni are a natural group of SVA investors. They usually have
special emotions for their Alma Mater, a fact that some education
institutions exploit very well. Today, alumni manifest their gratitude for
their Alma Mater through donations. If they had an option to increase,
even slightly, the return they obtain from their donations, wouldn't they
be willing to make it? Today, the only return they obtain from their
donations is the satisfaction of helping their Alma Mater, and perhaps
easier admission for their children. Therefore, they would probably be
willing to offer capital in the form of HCCs, helping the same number
of students – or more – and receiving an additional economic return.

Chapter 8 explains the multiplicative effect that switching from pure donations to HCCs can have on the amount of capital available for financing education.

Another natural group of SVA investors would include those who are interested in or passionate about a particular area of knowledge that is not necessarily economically profitable. These investors would be the equivalent of the Maecenas of earlier ages. People who today are fond of sponsoring art in all its forms are the most representative of this category. Other fields could be religious studies, pure mathematics, and philosophy.[14] As with the case of alumni, HCCs can increase the capital available for funding education in these areas by offering sponsors a small return instead of none.

A third group of SVA investors are those who support philanthropic causes. For example, the extra cost needed to provide education for handicapped individuals might make the investment, in pure economic terms, unprofitable. However, philanthropists, who today donate money without expecting returns, might be willing to provide even more funding if offered HCCs that could potentially generate some returns. Alternatively, they might be willing to offer the same funding, but it would benefit a larger number of students.

There can be many other types of SVA investors besides those described above. The common trait among all of them is their willingness to accept a lower return for the level of risk they are assuming by engaging in certain HCCs. Given the risk involved in HCCs while they are still a novel contract, perhaps the SVA investor will be the most common type in the beginning. However, as the knowledge surrounding HCCs increases and the risk for investors decreases, EVA investors should provide most of the capital in economically viable fields of study, with SVA investors providing capital in less-profitable fields.

EVA and SVA investors can also potentially combine with each other in funds with blended returns. In such funds, some investors can take on more risk than others. This can work, for example, between EVA investors and alumni of universities. EVA investors would perceive a smaller risk because alumni might be willing to invest taking more risk than them. SVA investors would see a multiplier effect from their efforts in the increased capital available from EVA investors.

EVA and SVA investors will have different needs and preferences with respect to returns. These preferences will be reflected in the grouping of students in the funds they invest in. As with investors, there are many possible ways that students can be combined. The market will create alternatives to satisfy different needs. Here are some likely possibilities.

Groups of students

Financial markets are always looking to structure instruments that permit them to schedule cash flows in a particular way, or to pool together independent assets of similar risk. As an example, imagine an investor who plans to retire in four years. To start receiving cash flows then, this investor might place money in a fund that invests in freshmen students only. In that way, when the students graduate and start earning money four years after, the investor starts to receive income from his investment just as he loses the income from his permanent job. Because the cash flow schedule from members of the same graduation class is similar, grouping students by academic class will help satisfy the needs of individuals planning for retirement, as well as insurance companies and other institutions that need to match their cash inflows with their outflows. Therefore, time to graduation is a natural way to pool students.

However, time to graduation groups are but one possible way to pool students. Another way of grouping students is by field of study. This would serve the interests of value investors, as well as those of investors who are interested in funding a particular area of knowledge regardless of its return. Presumably, the rate asked by investors of students in the same field group would be similar, reflecting the average earning statistics available for that profession. Grouping students by field reflects similarity in the risks and the expected returns within the same group. Companies are natural investors in pools of students grouped by field of study. By investing in these groups, companies can hedge against salary increments for employees who come from particular fields. The possible higher returns that companies would obtain from HCCs would help compensate for the increased compensation of their employees.

A third way to group students is by university. This group would be of particular interest to alumni who wish to help their Alma Mater. Grouping by university recognizes the potential for income generation due to the prestige of particular universities.

Since the characteristics of the returns between fields of study *and* universities are possibly different, the two groupings would probably happen simultaneously and pooling would occur by field of study and university (or cohort of universities). For example, a pool could be that of liberal arts students at Harvard. However, when grouping by university and career investors would be able to make only very small pools. Previously in this chapter I explained why that would not be desirable for the student or the investor. To solve this issue, the groupings may occur between similar groups of careers, and similar groups of universities. For example, rather than investing in liberal arts students at Harvard or Yale, investors might form a group of liberal arts students in all Ivy League universities. Although the risks and returns of this group of universities may not be exactly equal, they are similar enough to make of the cohort a better solution than having few students in a pool.

Other possible divisions may include geographic region, class rank, and other characteristics. One thing is for sure: if HCCs become popular there will be many more combinations than I can encompass in this book.

Securitizing the contract

The previous section discussed possible groupings of investors and students. In this section I will discuss securitization, a process by which investors in HCCs can achieve greater liquidity and reduced risk.

Asset securitization entails pooling specific kinds of assets (e.g. mortgages) together and dividing up claims to the pool into small fractions and selling these claims to investors. The process is analogous to stock issuance: claims to the net assets of a company are divided into small fractions and subsequently distributed among many investors.

In the previous section I described a process where different kinds of investors form groups according to their risk and return preferences; through securitization the process becomes one of different kinds of investors buying small portions of securitized HCCs. Hence, investors can shell out smaller quantities of cash than would otherwise be required from them. The greatest advantage, however, is the liquidity provided by small, easily tradable units. This will attract more capital and lower the cost of financing education for students.

When HCCs start to be traded in such a way, we will witness a decline in the illiquidity premium required by investors. Any kind of HCC, profitable or not, is a candidate for being traded – just as good and bad stocks are traded – as long as someone is willing to accept the first loss. Whereas EVA investors will scramble to invest in the most profitable fields of study, SVA investors will be willing to accept the losses from less-profitable contracts.[15] After an investor has borne the first loss, non-profitable contracts will fluctuate in value in the same way as profitable ones do.

This process resembles the movement of share prices after an initial public offering (IPO). The profitable companies end up trading at prices higher than the IPO price, while unprofitable companies end up trading at lower share prices. However, both profitable and unprofitable shares trade constantly. In the former case, original investors realize a gain while in the latter they realize a loss. The difference with HCCs investments is that SVA investors know beforehand that the contracts will not be profitable, but they invest anyway because they obtain satisfaction from sponsoring certain activities.

As I stated at the beginning of this chapter, the development of a market for HCCs as described above is more likely to materialize in countries with developed financial markets. In other countries adjustments would be needed for HCCs to be viable. Chapter 10 discusses some of those possible adjustments. Now we turn to why HCCs are the next logical step in financing education.

6 | *The case for human capital contracts*

I F traditional solutions adequately addressed the market failures in financing education, there would be no case for human capital contracts (HCCs).[1] However, because traditional solutions have not produced the desired results, a better alternative is needed. The discussion that follows addresses characteristics of HCCs that make them an attractive alternative for meeting the growing need for higher-education funding from private sources. The discussion is divided in two sections. The first addresses the advantages that income-contingent repayment schemes (ICRS) have over traditional mortgage-type contracts. HCCs, income-contingent loans (ICLs), and graduate taxes are ICRS, since the payments that students make are related to their income. The second section addresses the advantages HCCs offer that other ICRS do not.

The case for income-contingent repayment schemes

There are two main advantages of ICRS that make them superior to traditional mortgage-type loans. First, students reduce the risk they take when they invest in additional education; second, ICRS target educational subsidies, or payments below actual cost, to only those individuals who need them over a long period of time after graduation. These two advantages are described in more detail below.

Reduced income risk for students

As discussed in chapter 2, even though the *average* returns on education are high, the individual variance in the returns is also high. Ability and labor opportunities differ for each student. Moreover, there is the general threat of unemployment and incapacity. Faced with such prospects, it is not surprising that many potential students decide to join the labor market instead of pursuing additional education.

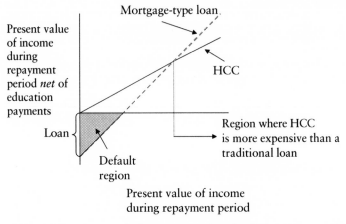

Figure 6.1 Income net of education payments for different types of instruments

ICRS decrease the risk for students by acting as a hedge against low or no income. As figure 6.1 shows, the range of a student's possible net earnings is narrower with an ICRS, in this case an HCC, rather than with mortgage-type loans.[2]

The dashed line in figure 6.1 represents the present value of a student's net earnings (total earnings minus education payments) under a mortgage-type loan. Because loan payments are independent of income, an increase in earnings implies an equal increase in net earnings – hence the 45-degree angle. When income is zero, net earnings will be negative, and will equal the loan payments. Of course, if income is actually zero, the student will not be able to pay her obligation and will default on her payments. Thus, the region in which net earnings are negative is depicted in figure 6.1 as the "default zone."[3]

The solid line in figure 1 represents the net present value (NPV) of net earnings under an HCC. This line differs from the mortgage-type loan line in two ways. First, because HCC payments represent a percentage of income, net earnings will never be negative. Net earnings are zero when income is zero (since payments would be zero), and increase proportionally with income. Second, the line is flatter than that of the mortgage-type loan. An increase in earnings does not translate into an equal increase in net earnings because payments increase proportionally as earnings increase. Thus, net earnings will increase, but at a slower rate than earnings.

These two differences illustrate the reduced risk a student faces under an HCC. First, because net earnings are never negative, the "default region" is greatly reduced. Second, the shallower slope of the HCC line illustrates that net earnings under an HCC are *less* sensitive to total earnings than net earnings under a mortgage-type loan. In other words, the student loses less if her earnings decrease, but also gains less if her earnings increase. Therefore, the present value of net earnings will be partially protected against variations in income.

Figure 6.1 also shows there is a point at which, for the same total earnings, net earnings are the same under both a mortgage-type loan and an HCC. For the student, this is the "break-even" earnings. At this point, the student gains nothing from going either way. If the student earns less, she is better off engaging in an HCC. On the other hand, if she earns more, she would have been better off with a traditional loan. Therefore, the advantages of engaging in HCCs come at a cost: the possibility of ending up with lower net earnings if total earnings during the repayment period turn out to be higher than the "break-even" total earnings. The advantages of an HCC have not been acquired without a cost; investors will bear risk for students only if they can gain something from it.

But the cost is borne only when the value of earnings is high. Assuming that a student is risk averse and that the expected value of payments (before knowing what the value of earnings end up being for the student) with an HCC and a loan are the same, the subjective expected value of engaging in an HCC is higher than that of the traditional loan. The value is a result of the student not knowing beforehand how high or low her earnings are going to be.

The risk reduction is especially important for low-income individuals and their families. The magnitude of the periodic payments that accompany a loan for education can easily overwhelm someone for whom a large portion of current income will go towards repayment. Considerations of future income expectations will pale in comparison to the psychological effect of *net* current income. Moreover, individuals who come from low-income families probably lack in their environment role models that exemplify the benefits of additional education. The result is a highly risk averse attitude towards such an investment. A proposition that permits students to finance their education *without* the risk of being unable to pay after obtaining their degrees should be appealing to low-income prospective students, making ICRS an excellent alternative for students with scarce individual and family resources to finance their education.

The creation of HCCs ultimately permits a risk transfer from students to investors. Such a market does not exist today, with the dire consequences described by Arrow:

> The nonexistence of markets for the bearing of some risks in the first instance reduces welfare for those who wish to transfer those risks to others for a certain price, as well as for those who would find it profitable to take on the risk at such a price, but it also reduces the desire to render or consume services which have risky consequences. (Arrow, 1971)

Therefore, by allowing a transfer of risk between students and investors, the welfare of students and investors who wish to transfer or take on risk is enhanced. As ICRS make education a less risky proposition, individuals are motivated to pursue additional studies, ultimately reducing under-investment in education.

Subsidy based on life-long needs

Traditional "means" tests for applying for scholarships or subsidies look closely at a student's background in search of an alternative source of capital for the student. Only those who prove that they really have no other option are offered scholarships. This is unfair for at least two reasons. First, some students from relatively wealthy families might be denied access to funds, even if their family is not willing to finance their education. Therefore, some students are unfairly marginalized from access to higher education just because of their family's decision. Second, some individuals from low-income backgrounds may build successful careers thereafter and be in a position easily to afford repaying the full cost of their education. In Barr's words:

> In the first place, the proposals [The government's proposal for a higher education financing program] focus on starting point rather than outcome. Lucky the shopworker's son who becomes a successful barrister, who pays no fees; unlucky the managing director's daughter who becomes a social worker. What matters is not where people start but where they end up. (Barr, 1998, p. 80)

Oosterbeek (1998) addresses this issue by pointing out the difference between static and dynamic equity. Under static equity principles, an individual's circumstances at a given point in time are the basis for decisions aimed at correcting inequality. If we follow our decisions by static equity criteria, we will give an educational subsidy to the student who is poor at the beginning of her studies, and let the wealthier one take care of herself. The principle of dynamic equity expands static notions to include the changes that happen over time. Following a principle of dynamic equity we would grant an educational subsidy to the *lifelong-poor* student, and let the *lifelong-rich* student take care of herself. Dynamic equity corrects for the limitations that short-term static-equity decisions have by including a time dimension to the decision of offering aid.

ICRS conform to a principle of dynamic equity, rather than to the "means" test principle of static equity. The payment that a student has to make adjusts dynamically to reflect changes in the student's earning power. ICRS provide a subsidy only to those individuals whose incomes are relatively low during the repayment period. Thus, an individual receives the subsidy based on the criteria of long-term need rather than on initial conditions. Anybody can apply for funding and only those who need a subsidy during their whole repayment period get it.

Conclusion: income-contingent repayment schemes

The importance of providing an alternative attractive to individuals who would otherwise have no other choice cannot be over-stated. Mincer (1974) shows in his book *Schooling, Experience and Earnings* how differences in education contribute to income inequality. Thus, giving a student a suitable alternative for financing education has implications for the distributions of income in society. Specifically, such an alternative would attack the differences in income resulting from unequal opportunities for accessing education.

ICRS allow students to make use of their future earnings to pay for their education. They do so without harming access to education since they reduce the risk of financial distress, reduce the risk of the return from the investment, and offer a targeted subsidy to those who face low life-long incomes.

ICLs – the ICRS that have received most attention since the 1960s – share all these advantages with HCCs over other private funding alternatives. However, HCCs have some additional characteristics that make them desirable over other ICRS. The following section describes these characteristics.

Beyond income-contingent repayment schemes: the case for human capital contracts

A measure for the value of education

If HCCs are freely traded, their pricing will relate educational costs and program lengths to future earnings.[4] Thus, the trading of these contracts will permit direct observation of the value of education that the market expects from the investment, illuminating different market expectations for different careers and universities. The *price* of the contract is the parameter in an HCC that will best capture market expectations of value and, from the student's point of view, it is the percentage of income committed per dollar financed. Having publicly available information on the value of education is especially important for at least two reasons: (1) it provides information regarding the quality of universities,[5] and (2) reveals contrasts among the values of different careers.

Quality comparison

Information on the value of education from different universities permits a comparison of the quality of education relative to its cost. The price of an HCC makes transparent the income expectations of the market for particular universities and fields of study. The result is heightened competition between universities, which creates pressures to improve the overall quality of education and to lower tuition costs.

Investors' interest in relating universities to earnings and costs would prompt the creation of independent rating agencies analogous to Moody's or Standard and Poor's but specializing in schooling returns. This generates more information for consumers, creating a market standard for improvement among higher-education institutions.

Ziderman and Albrecht state in *Financing Universities in Developing Countries* (1995) that one of the problems with providing students with traditional financing and leaving them to choose which university to attend induces them to go to universities where tuition is cheap rather than to universities that provide quality education. The incentive exists because the cheaper the university a student attends, the smaller the debt they end up with. In contrast, when engaging in HCCs, students will have an incentive to decide what university to attend based on the *total percentage* of income they have to commit rather than on the *absolute cost* of their education. The percentage of income they have to commit will depend on the relationship between future earnings, program length, and education costs of a particular university. Expensive universities whose alumni enjoy high postgraduate incomes will be at a disadvantage only if their incomes are not high enough to compensate for their educational costs. Thus, HCCs promote universities that offer cheap education *relative* to the incomes alumni enjoy (even if the costs are expensive in absolute terms), rather than cheap, low-future-income universities.

The results portrayed in appendix A (p. 167) clearly support this point. Equation (A.12) shows that the percentage of income that a student will have to commit is proportional to C/Y_s, where C is the amount financed and Y_s is the starting salary upon graduation. Higher costs (C) can be compensated by higher starting expected incomes (Y_s). Thus, assuming other factors (such as program length) constant, a student will have to commit the same percentage of income for an expensive university that has high-income prospects or for a cheap university with proportionally low-income prospects. The more expensive university will be a disadvantage only if it does not offer proportionally higher earnings.[6]

Furthermore, Ziderman and Albrecht (1995) emphasize that long programs make higher education unnecessarily expensive. Equation (A.12) in appendix A makes this point by showing that the percentages of income required by investors will grow exponentially with the time between the signing of the HCC and the entry of the student into the labor market. If universities can offer their students similar expected incomes upon graduation with *less* study time, then the cost for students will decrease exponentially. Thus, HCCs can potentially offer an incentive to those universities that can achieve the same education results in less time, recognizing the time-value of money for investors, and decreasing forgone earnings for students.

Relative value of careers

The pricing of HCCs would also permit direct comparisons between the relative values of different careers. Relative differences in HCC prices would provide signals to aid students in making career decisions. Whereas today information on expected compensation for different careers is available, students still need to offset those compensation figures against the costs (including the "time-value") of attending the university. Information on all these factors would be embedded in the pricing of HCCs, making the contrasts among careers more transparent. Presumably, the prices of HCCs would also more quickly reflect changes in the relative economic values of different careers, thus sending such information faster to the market.

The differences in the prices of HCCs would create an incentive for educational institutions to assign the real costs to each field of study. In most educational institutions, differences in tuition do not completely reflect the differences in the costs of providing education for a particular field of study. As a result, fields of study that are cheaper to deliver subsidize expensive ones. Increased transparency on the cost-benefit relationship of particular careers as reflected in the price of HCCs would create pressure from the students whose careers are subsidizing others to adjust costs appropriately. Universities that charge the real costs for each field of study would have an advantage over those that do not.[7]

An additional benefit of having direct information on the relative value of each career is the justification it provides for public expenditure on education. There is a case for government funding only those careers in which the benefits obtained by society are greater than those obtained by the individual.[8] Philosophy and the arts are commonly cited. HCC pricing will provide a market measure regarding *which* careers are unprofitable and *how much* is needed to make them profitable. Thus, resources that are used today to subsidize economically profitable careers can be used in a more efficient way by directing them exclusively to those careers whose social benefits are not captured by the incomes of individuals engaged in them.

Redistribution of outcomes

One more argument in favor of HCCs is the satisfaction of a distributive concept of fairness where economically successful students can bear higher payments, and students in financial difficulties are offered relief. HCCs demand less from low-income graduates and more from high-income graduates, whereas fixed payments represent a bigger burden for low-income graduates while being easier to cope with by high-income ones. Thus, HCCs correct the regressive effect of fixed payments: students who end up with higher incomes indirectly subsidize the smaller payments received from students with lower incomes.

Redistribution from individuals with higher incomes to those with lower incomes is typically an important goal for policymakers around the world. Not many instruments permit the pursuit of a policy goal – higher education – while at the same time pursuing another typical policy goal – less inequality – *without interfering with the outcomes of an open economy, but rather enhancing its efficiency.* Thus, HCCs satisfy a concept of fairness for a wide political spectrum. At one extreme, it appeals to those who see equality as a goal in itself. And at the other, it appeals to those who promote the workings of free markets.

Additional liquidity for investments in education

The individuals who invest in their own education cannot sell part of the value of their investment under traditional methods. Therefore such investment is an illiquid one. Low-liquidity investments, because of their nature, require higher rates of return than other investments that can be more easily traded. This feature of investments in education causes investors to discount education at higher rates than more liquid investments with similar risk profiles. A higher discount rate, given identical cash flows, translates into a lower NPV of the investment.

An active market where HCCs are traded enables individuals to "sell" part of their investment, making it more liquid. As a result, part of the "illiquidity premium" usually charged to investments in education would decrease. This, in turn, should cause the overall discount rate for investments in education to decrease. The final result is that while cash flows remain identical, the value of obtaining education increases.

HCCs would free part of the value of investing in education currently locked up by the limitations in its financing. An analogous concept in finance is that of the optimal amount of leverage that a firm should have. The theory states that any level of leverage that does not produce the minimum weighted average cost of capital (WACC) for the firm is not optimal because cash flows are discounted at a higher rate than they could be. The difference between the values obtained from discounting cash flows at the optimal discount rate rather than at the firm's actual discount rate represents an opportunity cost from using suboptimal leverage.

The same concept can be applied to investments in education. Current rigidities of the market do not allow individuals to minimize their "education discount rate," the effect being a lower value from investments in education. The increased NPV of investments in education brought about by their increased liquidity through HCCs is additional value produced for society.

An efficient alternative for philanthropy

The case for addressing under-investment in education goes beyond reaching the optimal level of investment. The impact that education has also relates to the philanthropic efforts against poverty. Whereas HCCs can help to attack poverty with solid economic incentives, they can also do so even when the investment is not economically profitable. I mentioned in chapter 5 that Social Value Added (SVA) investors could use HCCs. The value of this particular form of HCCs comes from its multiplicative effect.

To understand why HCCs multiply the capital available, consider an example in which a philanthropist donates $1,000 for someone's education. After completing her studies, the recipient of the gift enjoys the benefits on more education through higher average income over a lifetime. Unless the individual decides to share part of her higher income, the initial $1,000 donation ends there. If $1,000 are used in a HCC, the student who receives the gift is committed to sharing part of the extra income with the person or institution that made the donation. Thus, the $1,000 will generate a cash flow back to the original source. Since the donation presumably went to financing education where the private benefits did not offer satisfactory returns, the present value of the cash flow that returns to the philanthropist should on average be less than $1,000. As an example, assume that the present value is only $800. In that case, the "real" donation was of $200, and the remaining $800 can be used to finance four other $1,000 dollar education investments. The $1,000 that originally financed one investment can now finance five through HCCs.

The multiplicative effect comes from asking the beneficiaries of philanthropy – students – to share part of the benefits they enjoy from additional education with others. The philanthropist ends up aiding only as much as is needed to provide a market return for the investment.

In favor of income-contingent loans: the case against human capital contracts

HCCs have an *undesired* characteristic that ICLs do not have: i.e. students have the incentive for hiding and postponing income. Because the maximum amount that a student will pay is fixed and repayment periods are typically very long, ICLs are less prone to face this problem.

As a result, HCCs might face a higher rate of fraud than ICLs. This is so because (1) the pay-off of defaulting can be potentially much higher on an HCC than on an ICL and (2) postponing income can release individuals from their obligations. This is due to the design of these instruments: in the case of the HCC, the student might have to pay much higher amounts than the value of the original funding while in an ICL the student has to pay only up to the value of the loan.

While these concerns are valid, they can be addressed through the design of the contract. For instance, if the contract requires the student to submit his or her tax declaration, evading human capital payments by submitting false information would also imply submitting false information to the state: the risk of evasion becomes higher for the student. Income postponement can be addressed by explicitly stating in the contract that income derived from activities that the individual performed during the repayment period should be included in the calculation of payments, even if the income is received after the repayment period. For example, MyRichUncle's[TM][9] master funding agreement explicitly states:

The remainder of this section articulates the most common forms of compensation which shall be recognized as gross income; the parties agree, however, to amend this section as necessary to accommodate alternative forms of, and methods of receiving, compensation received by the student, so long as the compensation is the result of the student's productive efforts during the payment period. (MyRichUncle's[TM] Master Funding Agreement, section 12, part (a), paragraph (i))[10]

Further, the fact that ICLs have typically long repayment periods reduces the incentive to postpone and hide income. This would be specially true in the case of highly successful individuals who must remit an amount several times greater than what they originally received in funding. However, these individuals are few and are relatively easier to track, which should thus reduce the magnitude of the problem.

Capping the maximum payments that a student will make is prob-ably the best way to reduce the effect of these negative incentives. A cap would decrease the pay-off of defaulting, the pay-off of postpon-ing income, and the possibility of facing adverse selection. However, a cap limits the upside potential for investors, and thus takes away an important source of value for them and will presumably increase the price of the contract. The most important consequence of adding a cap, however, is the financial similarity of the resulting instrument to an ICL. (This is discussed in chapter 7.)

Appendix C (p. 184) contains tables that summarize the features and advantages of HCCs and ICLs compared to traditional "mortgage-type" loans.

7 | *Human capital options*

C HAPTERS 1–6 explored human capital contracts (HCCs), the history of the idea, how they would operate, and the reasons why their introduction was desirable for higher-education financing. This chapter introduces an additional instrument that can further enhance the use of future earnings to improve higher-education financing. The introduction of this instrument is a new insight brought forward in this book, as it creates a different framework for analyzing and implementing income-contingent loans (ICLs). It builds on options theory, in particular on their use for valuing contingent claims, to analyze the valuation and sources of risk within ICLs.[1] The instrument introduced here will be named a human capital option (HCO).[2]

Understanding that the reader might not be familiar with the theory of financial options, the following section is a short introduction about these instruments, and shows how they can be useful, before describing the HCO in particular.

What is an option?

An introduction

The kinds of options referred to in this book are financial options. A financial option gives its owner the right to buy, or sell, an asset at a predetermined price on, or before, a predetermined date. The particular conditions attached to an option are part of the jargon used every day by option traders. The most important are defined below.

The creation of an option takes place when two parties sign a contract in which one party – the *owner* of the option – gets the right to buy or sell an asset from the other party – the *writer* of the option. The price at which the asset can be bought or sold is the *strike price*, and the date at which the right expires is the *maturity date* of the option. If the option gives its owner the right to buy an asset, the option is called

Table 7.1 *The language of options*

Term	Definition
Owner	Has the right to buy or sell an asset
Writer	Has the obligation to sell or buy if the owner decides to exercise her right
Maturity date	The date at which the owner's right expires
Call	An option in which the owner has the right to buy an asset
Put	An option in which the owner has the right to sell an asset
Underlying asset	The asset that the owner of the option has the right to buy or sell
Strike price	The price at which the owner of the option has the right to buy or sell the underlying asset
Pay-off	The profit the owner makes when exercising her right
American option	An option in which the owner has the right to exercise her right at any moment on or before the maturity date
European option	An option in which the owner has the right to exercise her right only on the maturity date

a *call*; conversely, if the option gives its owner the right to sell an asset, the option is called a *put*. The asset that the owner of the option has the right to buy or sell is the *underlying asset* of the option. If the owner's right to buy or sell can be exercised at any moment before the maturity date, the option is an *American* option; otherwise, if the owner's right to buy or sell can be exercised only on the maturity date, the option is *European*. Finally, the gain made by the owner of the option when exercising it is called the *pay-off* of the option. Table 7.1 summarizes these definitions.

Let's consider an example of an option: An institution has the right to buy one share of Microsoft on August 26, 2003, at a price of $75 per share. This option is a call option because it gives the institution the right to buy shares. For this particular call option, the strike price is $75, the maturity date is August 26, 2003, and the underlying asset is Microsoft stock. The option is European because the institution has the right to exercise it only on the maturity date, not before.

On August 26, 2003, the institution that owns the option will decide whether or not to exercise its right, depending on the price of Microsoft stock. If Microsoft stock is trading for less than $75, the owner will not exercise the option, since doing so would entail buying one share of Microsoft for $75 while it can be bought in the market for less. On the other hand, if Microsoft's stock is trading for more than $75, then the owner will exercise the option, since by doing so it is acquiring for $75 a share that is more expensive in the market. For example, if the stock is trading at $80, the owner has an opportunity to make a profit by exercising the option, buying the share for $75 and immediately going to the market and selling it for $80. By exercising the option, its owner made a profit of $5 ($80 – $75). However, usually when an owner of an option exercises it, the writer of the option will give the profit from the operation – the pay-off of the option – directly to the owner of the option, rather than going through the process of buying the shares and then going out and selling them. In general, the pay-off from a call option will be the difference between the market price and the strike price of the underlying asset when the market price is higher than the strike price, and zero otherwise.

Some attractive attributes

The characteristics that options have make them appealing to investors in different circumstances. The attributes that are pointed out below are particularly relevant for our future discussion about ICLs.

First, notice that an option always has value. In the worst case, the owner will not exercise the option and lose nothing beyond the cost of acquiring the option. If things go well, then the potential pay-off can be very high. In general, having an option to do something always has to be valuable, since in some cases it can be exercised at a gain, and in the worst case, the option will yield nothing, leaving conditions identical to not having an option. A financial consequence of this property of options is that giving an option always entails giving away something valuable. Thus, the writer of an option should receive compensation for it, or else a loss will be generated.[3]

Another property that options give to their owners is protection against losses due to unfavorable changes in the value of the underlying asset, while the gains of favorable changes are retained.[4] Continuing the previous example, the institution that owns the option is protected against movements of the value of Microsoft stock below $75. When the stock price goes from $50 to $45, the pay-off to the owner of the option is not affected. However, when the stock moves from $90 to $100, the owner is affected, in a positive way.

Because of the protection they offer, options are used frequently as a tool for managing risk. They can be designed and combined with other assets in different ways depending on the kind of risk protection that the owner of the option seeks. Consider the following example of a combination of an asset and an option: a farmer interested in protecting his corn crop against low prices can buy an option to sell (a put) the crop at a given price. Notice that he is the owner of the crop, so he has an asset, and he is also the owner of the option, so he actually combines the possession of an asset with an option. If corn prices go down, he will at least receive the amount at which he has the right to sell. If corn prices go up, he will not exercise the option, but he will gain from the extra income he will receive because of the high prices. Thus, for the price at which he bought the option, this farmer got low-income protection and has guaranteed a certain minimum level of income. Many other examples could be thought of with different combinations of options and assets that would produce different risk-protection profiles.

A special option: human capital as the underlying asset

The potential for combining financial instruments to adjust to the particular risk preferences of different individuals and institutions makes options a very appealing financial instrument. The proposal discussed focuses on how to employ them to protect individuals against fluctuations in their income. In general, as low-income protection has become one of the most important social roles of governments throughout the world, the use of options to offer protection against low income has relevant implications for the way the management of these risks is thought about, handled, and valued. This book concentrates on financing higher education, and thus these options will be introduced as a tool to protect students. The study of other important applications is left for further research.

Chapter 2 pointed to the risk involved in investing in education as one of the reasons why financing education using traditional "mortgage-type" loans was so difficult. HCCs are described in chapters 4 and 5 as a way of managing that risk. HCOs are presented here as another, complementary, way of managing the risk of investments in additional education. The implementation of HCOs would provide alternatives and combinations that would translate into better ways for managing risks for students.

An HCO is defined here as an option in which the underlying asset is the value of the earnings that an individual receives as a result of his productive efforts during a given period of time. HCOs could be created as puts or calls, could have different maturity dates and different strike prices depending on the way risk would be managed using the option. Arrangements that resemble the pay-off of this kind of option exist today, but the instrument as such still does not exist.

Following the example of the farmer who, to protect himself against low corn prices combined his asset with an option to sell his crop at a fixed price, an individual could use a similar combination to protect himself against low income. In the farmer's case, the asset used to combine with the option was the crop; in the individual's case, her income can be used as the underlying asset. Thus, an individual can protect herself against low income by buying an option that gives her the right to sell her income at a given price. Acquiring such an option guarantees a minimum income level to the individual. An example of an option with these characteristics is discussed in the following subsection.

An example of a human capital option

Let's explore how an HCO could work. The first relevant parameter is the income that the individual wants to sell.[5] Is it one year's income? Ten years of income? Lifetime income? The answer to this question will depend on the needs of the individual and, in theory, options could be designed to satisfy each of these possibilities. As an example, assume that an individual wishes to buy an option for selling five years' worth of her income. The design of options for different lengths of time would follow a similar process to the one outlined below.

The second relevant parameter for estimating the value of income during a given period is the discount rate. Because the option is a contract between a buyer and a seller, the discount rate can be whatever value the seller and the buyer of the option are willing to accept. However, to estimate a fair value, the discount rate should reflect the risk involved in the income flows.[6] For the following example, a discount rate of 10 percent will be used.

Table 7.2 *Calculation of pay-off for human capital option: example 1*

| Year | Discount rate 10% | | | | |
	1	2	3	4	5
Income	100.000	100.000	100.000	100.000	100.000
Discounted value of income					
Income/(1 + discount rate)^{year} ($)	90.909	82.645	75.131	68.301	62.092
Value of income on year contract is signed (sum of discounted values of income) ($)	379.079				
Strike price ($)	300.000				

The third parameter is the strike price – the price at which the option owner has the right to sell her income. This is simply the minimum value the individual will receive for five years of income, and it should be defined as a given amount on a given date. For example, the strike price can be given as a value at the moment the option contract is signed, or it can be given as the value five years after the contract is signed. If the strike price is defined as a value at the moment the contract is signed, then the value of income should be estimated *discounting* the flows of the next five years. If the strike price is defined as a value five years after the contract is signed, then the value of income should be estimated *compounding* the income of the previous five years. For the example that follows, we will use a strike price of $300,000 at the moment the contract is signed.

Finally, the writer of this option is not willing to give the option to the individual for free. The individual will pay $5,000 when signing the contract for having the right to sell her income. This is the cost of the option.

Thus, the individual acquires for $5,000 an option that gives her the right to sell five years of her income, discounted at a 10 percent rate, for $300,000 measured in present value at the moment the option is bought. Now let's assume that the individual had an income of $100,000 a year during those five years. Table 7.2 (example 1)

Table 7.3 *Calculation of pay-off for human capital option: example 2*

Year	Discount rate 10%				
	1	2	3	4	5
Income	70.000	70.000	70.000	70.000	70.000
Discounted value of income					
Income/(1 + discount rate)^{year} ($)	63.636	57.851	52.592	47.811	43.464
Value of income on year contract is signed (sum of discounted values of income) ($)	265.355				
Strike price ($)	300.000				

summarizes the operations that follow that show if this individual will exercise her option after five years or not.

After five years, the value of the individual's income, estimated at the time the contract was signed, adds up to $379,080. She has the right to sell that amount for $300,000, but of course will not do it as her income was worth more than that and she would lose $79,080 if she did exercise her option. In this case, the individual paid $5,000 to acquire the right to sell her income, and this right turned out to be worthless after five years.

But now consider another example, identical in every parameter to the previous one, except that this time the individual earns only $70,000 a year. The calculations to estimate the pay-off of this option are shown in table 7.3 (example 2).

In this example the individual will exercise her right to sell her income for $300,000, since the value of five years' of income was only $265,355. The individual will go to the writer of the option and receive $300,000 in exchange for $265,355. The individual ends up with $300,000 and the writer of the option with a loss of $34,645 ($300,000 – $265,355) before considering the cost of the option. Thus, by using an HCO and paying $5,000, the individual achieved her original purpose of ensuring a minimum income after five years.

One final adjustment remains to be made: the analysis shown in table 7.2 and table 7.3 would presumably be made in the fifth year, since the individual's income would not be known when the signing of the contract took place. Since the amounts calculated above are estimated in present value terms at the signing of the contract (year 0), an adjustment has to be made to calculate their present value in the fifth year. This is done by compounding $300,000 and $265,355 for five years at a rate of 10 percent ($300,000 $\times$ 1.1^5 and $265,355 $\times$ 1.1^5, respectively). The results, $483,153 and $427,357, are used as the strike price and the value of income on the fifth year.

Using these new values, in the fifth year the individual receives $483,153 in exchange for $427,357 making a profit of $55,796 ($483,153-$427,357) before considering the cost of the option. Likewise, the writer of the option makes a loss of $55,796. Notice that $55,796, the amount that the writer loses equals the loss calculated for the year the contract was signed ($34,645) compounded for five years at a rate of 10 percent (that is, $55,796 = $34,645 $\times$ 1.1^5). Thus, in the second example the right that the individual bought to sell five years' worth of income ended with a value of $55,796 at the end of the five years. For a low cost, the individual protected herself against having a low income.

These examples show how HCOs could be implemented to offer low-income protection for individuals. Notice that the protection achieved came from combining the option – the right to sell income – with an asset – the individual's income, in the same way that the farmer obtained protection by combining an option – the right to sell the crop at a given price – with an asset – the crop. The following discussion goes one step further and analyzes what could be done if the asset and the option are combined with a loan. The result can be employed as protection against default on the loan, a very desirable attribute for the design of higher-education loans.

One step further: a human capital option, an asset, and a liability

The previous discussion shows how HCOs could be used to protect individuals against low income. Chapter 2 pointed out that the uncertainty in a student's future income was one of the major sources of market failure in the financing of higher education through traditional "mortgage-type" loans. This section introduces the use of HCOs as a mechanism to bridge the uncertainty in a student's future income and the use of loans to finance education.

The examples explored above offered the individual certainty on a minimum level of income after the pay-off of the option had been received. One reason why individuals might be interested in guaranteeing a minimum income, besides providing for basic life necessities, is to be able to pay for obligations previously acquired as loans. In particular, if an individual is planning to incur debt to finance additional education, low-income protection can offset a disappointing result from that investment. On the other hand, the lender providing the loan would perceive a lower risk if the minimum income level of the individual is guaranteed. Thus, an HCO could be used in this case to satisfy the protection needs of the individual and the lender.

An example of a human capital option and a loan

Let's consider a student who wants to protect herself against the possibility of not being able to pay her student loan. The loan is a flexible loan that allows the student to pay whatever she wants, as long as after five years any balance on the loan and accrued interest is repaid. The student does not want to pay a big amount at the end of the fifth year, and so decides to pay 10 percent of her income each year, and pay the remaining balance at the end of the life of the loan. But to protect herself against having to make a large payment on the fifth year to cover the remaining balance, she decides to buy an HCO. Although she could protect her whole income, she decides that this is more protection than she needs, and that she really wants to cover only a fraction of her income required to pay the loan. Since the student decided to use 10 percent of her income every year, it is reasonable for her to seek protection against fluctuations in 10 percent of her income. Therefore, the option that this student needs is one that gives her the right to sell 10 percent of her income over five years at the value of the loan and accrued interest. Such an option ensures that 10 percent of her income is enough to repay the loan and that at the end of five years the student does not have to make any further payments, as the pay-off of the option will always be equal to the balance owed after five years.

To make the previous point clear, let's assume that the loan was for $40,000, payable in five years, with an interest rate of 10 percent. Also

Table 7.4 *Example payments and loan balance calculations*

Year	1	2	3	4	5
1 Loan balance beginning of year ($)	40.000	34.000	27.400	20.140	12.154
2 Interest accrued during year (10% of balance at beginning of year) ($)	4.000	3.400	2.740	2.014	1.215
3 Balance at end of year (1 + 2) ($)	44.000	37.400	30.140	22.154	13.369
4 Student income ($)	100.000	100.000	100.000	100.000	100.000
5 Payment (10% of income) ($)	10.000	10.000	10.000	10.000	10.000
6 Loan balance after payment (3 − 5) ($)	34.000	27.400	20.140	12.154	3.369

assume that the student's income was $100,000 over five years, and that the strike price on the option was $40,000 at the moment the contract was signed. The discount rate that will be used to calculate the present value of income is 10 percent. The fact that the strike price and the value of the loan are the same is no coincidence, this is how the student makes sure that 10 percent of her income is enough to pay for the loan. Further, the discount rate and the interest rate of the loan have to be the same, otherwise the student will not get *exactly* the amount needed to make sure that 10 percent of her income during five years pays her loan.

Table 7.4 shows the payments that the student would make each year and the balance owed at the end of the year. On this example, the student would owe $3,369 at the end of the fifth year. According to her loan obligation, she would have to pay this amount in the last year.

But the student also has an option to sell 10 percent of her income for $40,000. Table 7.5 (example 3) shows the calculation of the pay-off of the option after five years. The present value of 10 percent of income is $37,908, which means that the student will exercise her right to sell 10 percent of her income for $40,000. In doing so, she will receive the difference between $40,000 and $37,908, or $2,092. This amount is measured in present value terms at the time the contract was signed.

Table 7.5 *Calculation of pay-off for Human Capital Option: example 3*

	Discount rate 10%				
	---	---	---	---	---
Year	1	2	3	4	5
10% of income ($)	10.000	10.000	10.000	10.000	10.000
Discounted value of 10% income					
Income/(1 + discount rate)^{year} ($)	9.091	8.264	7.513	6.830	6.209
Value of income in year contract is signed (sum of discounted values of income) ($)	37.908				
Strike price ($)	40.000				

On the fifth year this amount equals $3,369 ($2,092 × 1.1^5). As can be seen, *the pay-off of the option equals exactly the loan balance that the student would still owe in the fifth year.* In the fifth year the student can use the pay-off of the option to cover the balance on the loan.

Example 3 shows that an HCO can be combined with an asset – a percentage of student's income – and with a liability – the loan – to ensure that a percentage of income will be enough to repay back the loan. In other words, using an HCO protects the debtor against low income to pay back her liabilities. Such a combination should be attractive for students, whose future income is the one that allows them to pay back their student debts.

This example used an HCO, giving the owner the right to sell her income at a given price. The following section explores another possible combination of HCOs, this time options that give the owner the right to buy her income at a given price.

A different combination: a human capital contract and a human capital option

The implementation of HCCs would also create an opportunity for the existence of a different kind of HCO. In a world where HCCs are widely used, the students who take them face the risk of paying a disproportionate amount of money if they are economically very successful. Thus, students might be interested in being protected against paying high amounts for their success.

Chapters 4 and 5 pointed out that an HCC is the economic equivalent of a student selling a percentage of her future income. If the student is economically very successfully after joining the workforce the student would have sold that percentage of her income cheaply. The corresponding protection against this circumstance would come from an option to buy back that part of income at a given price. The individual buys an option that gives her the right to purchase a percentage of her income at a predetermined value. The student would buy back her own income at the strike price if the value of her income ended up being worth more than the strike price.

Let's repeat the previous example, but this time assuming that the student entered into an HCC and into an HCO. To make the values comparable, this student engaged in an HCC in which she committed 10 percent of her income during five years in exchange for US$40,000. To protect herself against making high payments to the investors, she buys an option to buy 10 percent of her five-year income for $40,000. The interest rate that would be used to estimate the value of income is 10 percent. Upon graduation, the student receives a yearly salary of $100,000. Since all the numerical values are identical to the previous example, table 7.5 already shows the present value of 10 percent of the student's income. Notice that this corresponds to the value of the payments made to the investor of the HCC.

After five years the value of the payments that the student made to the investor of the HCC are worth $37,908. The student will not exercise her right to buy 10 percent of her income for $40,000, as she would be paying $40,000 for something worth only $37,908. In this case, the option the student bought expired without value, which means that rather than selling 10 percent of her income cheap to the investor of the HCC, the student sold 10 percent of her income for a higher value than it was worth.

Now let's look at what would have happened if the student had a higher income each year. For example, assume that her income was $120,000 a year upon graduation. Table 7.6 (example 4) shows the present value of 10 percent of her income and compares it to the strike price of the option to buy 10 percent of her income.

Table 7.6 *Calculation of pay-off for human capital option: example 4*

Year	Discount rate 10%				
	1	2	3	4	5
10% of income ($)	12.000	12.000	12.000	12.000	12.000
Discounted value of payments					
Payment/(1 + discount rate)^{year} ($)	10.909	9.917	9.016	8.196	7.451
Value of 10% income on year contract is signed					
(sum of discounted values of income) ($)	45.489				
Strike price ($)	40.000				

In this case, the value of the payments that the student made to the investor exceeded $40,000, and thus she ended up selling cheap 10 percent of her income. But because the student has an HCO, she has the right to buy back 10 percent of her income for $40,000. As a result, the student ended up paying, in present value terms, $40,000 ($45,489 paid to the investors and income received of $5,489 from the writer of the option), fulfilling the purpose of protecting herself against high payments.

Human capital options: a graphical approach

So far the analysis of HCOs has been done with the help of numerical examples. It might be helpful now to perform the same analysis using a graphical approach. Using this method will aid the reader in having a mental picture of the effect that the HCOs are having on the amounts that the student has to pay to lenders or to investors in HCCs.

First, consider the option that gives the individual the right to sell a percentage of income. As discussed in the previous examples, the pay-off of this option will depend on the relationship between the present value of the individual's income and the strike price of the option. The individual will make a gain as long as the percentage of income that she has the right to sell is worth less, in present value terms, than the strike

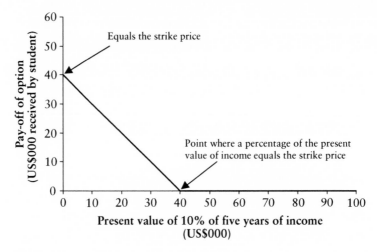

Figure 7.1 Pay-off of a human capital option that gives the student the right to sell a percentage of her income

price. Further, the value of the gain will equal the difference between the strike price and the present value of the percentage of her income she has the right to sell. Once the present value of the percentage of her income is higher than the strike price, the student does not make any gain, and the right to sell her income is worthless. This relationship is depicted graphically in figure 7.1.[7] The numbers correspond to the example analyzed above of an option that gives the student the right to sell 10 percent of five years of her income for $40,000.

Now consider what happens when this pay-off is combined with the value of payments the student makes to repay a loan. Because these payments are independent of income, the line in figure 7.1 will be displaced downwards by the amount paid by the student. Figure 7.2 shows the example analyzed above in which a student combines the right to sell 10 percent of five years of her income for $40,000 and has a loan for $40,000.

Figure 7.2 can be generalized to any combination of an HCO and a loan, as long as the value of the loan equals the strike price of the option. This graph shows the effect of the option on the loan: it reduces net payments should income fall below a certain threshold, thus offering low-income protection.

Now let's analyze the other combination discussed above, an HCC and an HCO. Let's consider first the payments that the student will

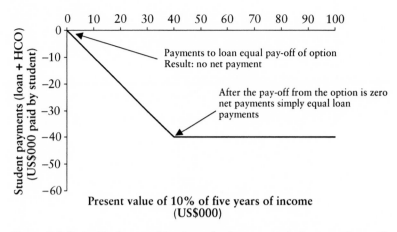

Figure 7.2 Pay-off of a combination of a human capital put option and a loan

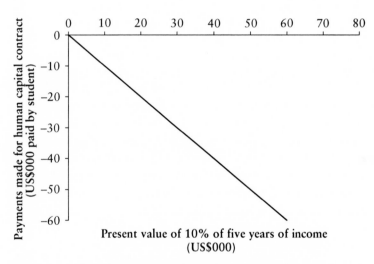

Figure 7.3 Value of payments made in a human capital contract

have to make to the investors who provided the capital in the HCC. The value of these payments will start from zero when the student has no income, and will increase proportionally as the present value of income increases. This relationship is shown in figure 7.3 for the particular example in which a student agrees to pay 10 percent of her income during five years after graduation.

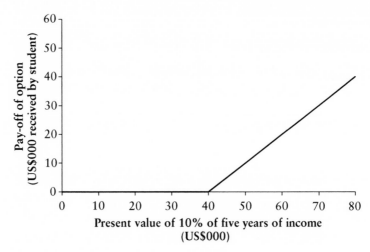

Figure 7.4 Pay-off of a human capital option that gives the right to buy a percentage of income

Now let's analyze the pay-off of an HCO that gives the student the right to buy a percentage of her income. As long as the present value of income is less than the strike price the option has no effect on the payments that the individual makes, since the pay-off of the option is zero (the individual will not buy a percentage of her income for more than it is actually worth). However, once the value of the percentage of income exceeds the strike price, the student makes a gain, since she is able to buy for the strike price something that is worth more than that. The gain will increase proportionally to an increase in the value of the individual's income. This behavior is shown in figure 7.4 using as an example an option that gives the student the right to buy 10 percent of the value of 10 percent of five years of her income for $40,000.

The payments that will result from combining an HCC with an HCO like the one depicted in figure 7.4 can be calculated simply by subtracting the pay-off of the option to the payments of the HCC. If the percentage of income that is committed to the HCC equals the percentage of income that can be bought through the HCO, then total payments that the individual will have to make are depicted in figure 7.5.

The effect that the option has on the total payments the individual makes can be interpreted as capping the total amount that will be paid

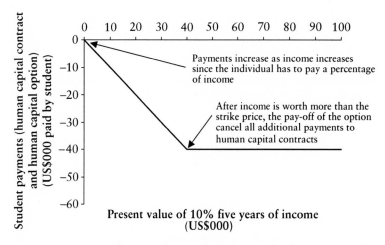

Figure 7.5 Payments from combining a human capital call option and a human capital contract

to the HCC. Thus, this option offers protection against high payments because of high income.

The most interesting aspect of the combination of a loan and a put HCO, and the combination of an HCC and a call HCO, is that the total payments that the individual will have to make with either method are identical! In other words, the financial outcomes of combining a put option and a loan, or combining an HCC and an HCO, are two different views of the same situation. Intuitively this is logical, since the put provides protection against low income in order to pay a fixed obligation; and the HCC provides protection against high payments to pay for a variable obligation. The net result is the same.[8]

In either case, to protect herself either against low income or against high payments, the individual probably had to pay for acquiring that protection. The cost of the protection, the cost of the option, will be such that, *on average*, it allows the writer of the option to make a profit. Therefore an HCO is not free: it has a cost in the same way that insurance coverage has a cost. But through HCOs individuals could have the choice of deciding whether they face the risk of not having enough income or purchase protection should they have difficult times.

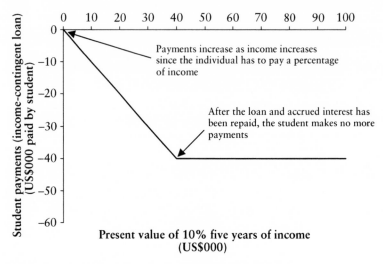

Figure 7.6 Payments made to an income-contingent loan

The relationship between human capital options and income-contingent loans

The beginning of this chapter stated that the introduction of HCOs would create a different framework for analyzing ICLs. After studying how HCOs would work and how they could be used with loans or with HCCs to protect student against low income or high payments, this section points out why this is relevant for ICLs.

ICLs have been gaining popularity for the reasons outlined in chapters 4 and 6, namely, they adjust to the capacity of the student to pay. A typical ICL requires a student to pay a percentage of her income until the value of the loan and accrued interest is paid or until the maximum repayment period is reached. If the student's income during the repayment period is not high enough to repay the loan and interest, the remaining balance is forgiven. This is a fundamental property of ICLs: students may not repay the complete value of the loan. This is true regardless of how long the repayment period is; even if the repayment period is a lifetime, some students will have low life-long incomes that will not be enough to repay the loan. Figure 7.6 shows the payments a student will make to an ICL as a function of income.

The relationship between ICLs and HCOs becomes transparent when figure 7.2, figure 7.5, and figure 7.6 are compared. The important insight *is that the value of the financial payments related to an ICL are exactly the same as engaging in a loan and in a human capital put option, and also exactly the same as engaging in an HCC and in a human capital call option!*

This relationship will also hold for ICLs in which students pay *each* period (typically a month) a percentage of their income up to a certain value, beyond which they pay a fixed amount. These ICLs are used in Chile, and were used in the program started by Harvard in 1971 (see Johnstone, 1972). The analysis is almost identical, except that in this case the student acquires one HCO per period, since the student is protected each period against not having enough income to pay a fixed payment. Appendix 2 develops this idea with additional detail.

The implications of creating human capital options

Separating ICLs into two instruments – loans and HCOs – offers enhanced flexibility for the design of private funding of higher education. In particular, combinations of loans and HCOs permit the transfer of risk to those investors in the market who have appetite for it.

In the past, discussion of the alternatives of implementing ICLs has focused on who pays the subsidy given to life-long low-income earners. The traditional answer has divided ICLs in two categories: externally subsidized and mutualized.[9]

Externally subsidized ICLs leave in hands of a third party – government, education institutions or other – the risk for any amount of the loan that students do not repay. Mutualized loans, in contrast, place the burden of the risk on a pool of students who are taking the loan. Australia's Higher-Education Contribution Scheme (HECS) program (see chapter 9) is an example of an externally subsidized ICL and Yale's Tuition Postponement Program (TPP) an example of a mutualized ICL.[10]

In the case of externally subsidized ICLs, separating the instrument into a loan and an HCC allows the entity (a lender) who is assuming the risk on repayments to transfer it to other parties. Simply "buying" an HCO such as the one described on p. 89 can transfer the risk. This transaction permits governments or institutions to acquire the option immediately, and thereafter face no uncertainty on the repayment of the loan because of life-long low incomes.

Mutualized ICLs appear very unattractive once ICLs are divided between loans and HCOs. Mutualized ICLs were designed by the institutional lenders to impose repayment risk on the pool of students. Because institutions had no effective way to transfer the risk to other parties their alternatives were limited to pooling students and letting some students assume the losses generated by others.

Johnstone (1972) analyzed several methods to charge high-income earners for the losses caused by low-income earners. One method is lending at a higher than market interest rate, with the unwelcome consequences analyzed in appendix B (p. 175). Another method is paying a factor of the original loan or of the original amount plus an interest rate. Yale's Tuition Postponement Program was one of the latter kind, with a maximum repayment of 150 percent of loan plus interest.[11]

These methods were successful in transferring the risk to the students. But the methods generated adverse reactions, since students didn't necessarily feel that it was fair for them to carry the obligations of other students, even if only up to a cap. A particularly vicious consequence of the perceived unfairness of this mutualized ICL is the incentive it creates for defaulting after other students decide to default on their obligations. The incentive exists because the students remaining in the system have to continue paying as long as the pool of students has debt outstanding, *even when other students in the pool are not honoring their obligation.* Once some members of a mutualized loan default, the students remaining in the pool have to pay for them. Thus, students who honor their obligations pay for those who do not.

The separation of ICLs into loans and HCOs makes mutualized loans unnecessary. If the ICL is not going to be externally subsidized – that is, if it is expected that students somehow cover for the low-income protection that is being offered to them – students simply need to be charged for the value of the option they have. The entity that is giving the loan can then choose to take the risk on the HCO or transfer it to someone else in the private market.[12]

As an example, assume that students are offered $1,000 through an ICL with a market interest rate and that the value of the option is estimated to be worth $200. The entity would give the student $800, but the student would have to pay back $1,000. The lending institution would then transfer the risk to the market by "buying" HCOs in the market for $200. The result is that students pay for the life-long income protection offered by the ICL in a way that *is not dependent on the results other students from their generation obtain* and the lending institution does not take the risk of life-long low incomes. Any amount that the student does not pay to cover the value of the option is an external subsidy given to the student.

Thus, the relevant questions for ICLs are who pays for the value of the option and who takes the risk on the pay-off of it. Today's alternatives permit only lenders or a pool of borrowers to take the risk while the introduction of HCOs would permit lenders, borrowers, or *the market* to assume the risk.

The value that HCCs can bring forward rests in the creation of a market for valuing human capital and derivatives that have human capital as the underlying asset. The design of existing ICLs required estimates on the value of human capital but did not allow the market to trade them. Separating an ICL into components, an HCC and an option or a loan and an option, can permit markets to price and trade the instruments separately. This would give more flexibility to implement future education financing programs, offer more choices to students, improve the alternatives that investors have for trading risk, and increase the information available on the value of education. The final result is more opportunities for those whose current financing constraints prevent them from making an investment in education to find ways to face the risks of continuing their educational development.

Nerlove (1972, 1975) explicitly recognizes ICLs as loans with low-income insurance. However, the idea of separating the loan from the insurance did not seem to be part of his discussion. This chapter points towards separating those two distinct instruments – the loan and the low-income insurance – as the answer to solving the problem of financing ICLs. Options theory can then be applied to determine the value of the insurance.[13]

Finally, the creation of HCOs would move towards building the products that Merton (1998) speculates can develop from the growing trend of incorporating option valuation into different fields:

Those products and services will include not only the traditional attempt to achieve an efficient risk-return trade-off for the tangible-wealth portfolio but will also integrate human-capital considerations, hedging and income and estate tax planning into the asset-allocation decisions. (Merton, 1998, 342)

Indeed, HCOs can integrate human capital considerations into asset allocation decisions.

III Implementing human capital contracts

8 | *Hurdles in the implementation of human capital contracts*

T HIS chapter addresses the practical problems of implementing human capital contracts (HCCs). Understanding the hurdles that must be surpassed requires us to understand those that were presented in the past and those that are valid today.

The hurdles of the 1960s: problems of the past

In theory, HCCs should be financially viable, i.e. they should attract investors and students. Nevertheless, the implementation of this particular kind of contract requires passing several hurdles. Milton Friedman recognized some of them in 1962:

There seems no legal obstacle to private contracts of this kind, even though they are economically equivalent to the purchase of a share in an individual's earning capacity and thus to partial slavery. One reason why such contracts have not become common, despite their potential profitability to both lender and borrower, is presumably the high costs of administering them, given the freedom of individuals to move from one place to another, the need for getting accurate income statements, and the long period over which the contracts would run. (Friedman, 1962, 103)

However, most of these concerns do not hold, because (1) HCCs are not partial slavery, (2) administration costs have decreased dramatically, and (3) financial markets today accommodate extremely long-term instruments.

Human capital contracts are not partial slavery

I will argue here that HCCs, even if they are the economic equivalent of selling a right to one's future income, do not amount to slavery or servitude. Far from enslaving individuals, HCCs are designed to permit them to exploit their full potential by allowing them to pursue the career of their choice without the burden of a fixed loan payment. The essence of slavery is the suppression of the slave's will in acquiescence to the master. As long as a contract or arrangement does not result in the suppression of an individual's will, there is no valid charge for slavery. Only if the contrary is true does a problem exist.[1]

The difference between what is proposed here and slavery rests entirely on the difference between human capital understood as the work that someone can do, and human capital understood as the value that an individual's production has. Traditionally, the lack of this distinction has led to the conclusion that human capital cannot be traded in a non-slave society. Blaug's description of the difficulty of financing investments in education offers an example:

In a non-slave society, the individual is his own property and this property is inalienable: he cannot give a lien on his services or make an enforceable contract to deliver his services for any considerable time in the future. Thus, non-slave societies lack capital markets in which rights to future earning power can be traded or in which the promise of earning power can be used as collateral for purposes of borrowing education finance. (Blaug, 1970, 4)

He states again later:

After all, capital markets are simply markets which convert income into capital and capital into income, that is, convert the promise of a flow of future payments into a single advance payment and vice versa. Because a non-slave society prohibits people from contracting to deliver their future services, "free" people must keep their human wealth tied up in the form of labour services and cannot hedge against unforeseen changes in the future demand for their services. (Blaug, 1970, 7)

But Blaug's statements are true only under the assumption that the rights to future earning power entail forcing the individual to deliver future services. That is, they are true only when we are assuming that the market for human capital trades services that an individual will perform. This assumption is true in some contracts (which Blaug mentions), such as those that force an athlete to play for a particular club for a specified period of time. But this assumption does not always have to be true. It is not true, for instance, if we understand the market for human capital as a market where *the value* of an individual's earnings is traded, regardless of what the individual decides to do. This would be the case for HCCs as they are described and argued for in this book. Rights to future earnings can be traded without forcing the individual to do anything in the future, allowing for the existence of a market where the trade of human capital – the value of an individual's future earnings, not the provision of services – takes place in a "free" society. Unfortunately, the idea that a market for human capital and a "free" society are incompatible has prevailed among economists who write about the topic. However, as long as the individual is free to decide what to do, the case against trading the value of human capital cannot be grounded in slavery or servitude.

A monetary obligation, whether fixed or variable, does not suppress the will of an individual. As long as the individual is free to choose where and how to work and live, giving a third person the right to a percentage of her future income does not restrain her will, not even *partially*. It can happen that an individual who has a fixed repayment obligation may be under more pernicious conditions than one whose obligation is variable if the terms of the fixed repayment scheme give the lender the right to dictate what the borrower can do. As stated in chapter 6, HCCs are designed such that the student remains the sole decision-maker when it comes to what to do with her life.

It might also be argued that slavery exists even when the will of an individual is not directly involved – as, for instance, in contracts where lenders are entitled to the production or earnings of another human being. This definition of slavery openly contradicts principles of modern capitalist societies. Every manufacturing company has the right to sell the production of its workers, and every loan implicitly grants the lender the right to the earnings of the borrower, *up to the amount of the loan*. In a mortgage-type loan, the borrower carries a burden the magnitude of which is a function of her income: when her income is high, mortgage payments pose a smaller burden; when her income is low, mortgage payments pose a heavier, perhaps unbearable, burden. In an HCC, just like in a loan, the provider of capital obtains a claim over the individual's earnings. The difference is that in an HCC, the burden of repayment is fixed, which some individuals may find more convenient.

Following Marshall's logic, "The worker sells his work, but he himself remains his own property" (Marshall, 1956/1890, 466), it can be said of HCCs that a student sells part of her income, but she herself remains her own property. As long as the rules by which an agreement between two parties are clear and legitimate, concerns about slavery or indentured servitude can be addressed by emphasizing the existence of a contract that describes the investor's and student's obligations which, in this case, do not include an obligation of the student to perform certain kinds of services. Finally, in the absence of personal or familial wealth, it is the performance of one's post-graduation services (the *sale thereof*) that will be used to pay for one's collegiate career, whether through payment on student loans or remittance to investors of their share of the income derived from those services.

The most striking modern example of a legitimate claim to a fraction of an individual's earnings is that of income taxes. The claim of the state lasts as long as the individual earns income, going beyond the claims of most traditional loans and the proposed repayment period for HCCs. Thus, there should not be a concern about claims covering the whole productive life of the individual. Although some taxpayers do actually feel like slaves, public opinion does not have a negative "indentured servitude" attitude towards this kind of taxation. There is no such attitude because states do not go around forcing individuals to work as a way of maximizing their tax revenues.

Because HCCs do not suppress the will of the student, and because they make a claim that is considered legitimate in capitalistic societies, they should be considered ethically acceptable. There is a possibility, however, that investors may misuse them by creating undue pressure on students. This is not peculiar to HCCs, however, since lenders can also create undue pressure on borrowers in traditional mortgage-type loans. But because the threat of suasion exists, contracts have to be designed in such a way as to avoid them.

The risk of investors exerting undue pressure on students can be managed by creating a significant distance between the investor and the student. This condition should be explicitly stated in the contract and will happen naturally if students are pooled in large groups. Pooling large numbers of students together prevents the investor from tracking one student in particular and, at the same time, reduces the impact of a single student's performance on an investor's investment. These two effects make it costlier for the investor to put pressure on a particular student. Thus, the securitization of HCCs is the main feature that will protect students.

In countries with developed markets, the process of securitization might happen naturally. However, in emerging and developing countries, where securitization may be difficult, other alternatives for the protection of students will have to be sought. One alternative is to place the state between the student and the investor. This option is explored further in chapter 11.

Technology has changed

Friedman's second objection – administrative costs – can be divided in two: those related to tracking individuals and those related to collecting payments. Tracking costs has changed dramatically since the date of Friedman's essay. Computers have cut to a fraction the costs of tracking individuals and the amount they owe. Thanks to powerful machines this technical hurdle can be vaulted. The hurdle of collecting still stands, and will be addressed later.

Financial markets provide liquidity to long-term contracts

The last concern raised by Friedman, the long period over which the contracts run, can be addressed by the demand that the development of financial markets has created for long-term contracts. There are several participants in the market interested in long-term obligations, such as life insurance companies and pension funds. *As long as the instrument can be easily traded*, there should not be any concern about its maturity.

Thus, of Friedman's arguments, only collection of payments remains as a hurdle. However, besides this, other challenges exist today that must be addressed to successfully implement HCCs.

Today's hurdles: challenges for the twenty-first century

Today, HCCs still face other ethical and financial objections besides those that were raised in the last section. In the light of what has been said before, can HCCs be designed in a legitimate way? Can they be implemented in a way that satisfies the financial requirements of students and investors? The following sections attempt to answer these questions.

Ethical concerns

I already explained why the main ethical objection to HCCs, that of slavery or indentured servitude, should not be an issue. There are, however, other ethical objections that have to be addressed now. The first objection is that HCCs can be discriminatory. The second is that they are unfair because of the unlimited upside potential. The third objection questions whether HCCs can protect students' rights. The following section explores all these.

Discrimination

Investors are likely to offer different contract terms for different careers and universities. Even for a given university, there could be different terms for students with different profiles. The argument for considering these differences unethical is discrimination.

But discrimination is, by definition, arbitrary. In the case of HCCs, differences in contract terms will reflect economic expectations – rather than personal prejudices. Thus there is no arbitrariness in the process. Further, as explained in chapter 8, the fact that contract terms will vary introduces competitive forces into the tuition universities charge for different careers and among the institutions themselves. Inhibiting the possibility of offering different contract terms for different careers and universities would destroy one of the fundamental strengths of HCCs.

Today, the alternative is worse. Students who take a "mortgage-type" loan face different burdens (as percentage of income), depending on their career and university. For example, if an artist and a lawyer paid the same tuition to attend the same university and they both financed their studies through "mortgage-type" student loans, the artist would probably have a higher effective burden than the lawyer, since artists have lower salaries on average than lawyers. The differences in burden between artists and lawyers would not be evident with "mortgage-type" loans, but HCCs would make the differences explicit, giving information beforehand to individuals who are deciding what career to choose and what university to attend.

Probably the most notorious case of differing contract terms will be those offered to individuals of different gender, race, or socio-economic background. For example, women might be offered more expensive conditions than men, based on lower expected income. But women's lower expected income is often the result other factors such as pregnancies and motherhood.[2] These differences are manifest today as higher debt burdens as a percentage of income for women than for men. This "unfair" practice is due to different income profiles that in turn are due partly to arbitrary reasons. As explained in the previous paragraph,

HCCs would make these differences explicit and much easier to measure and compensate.

Even though HCCs reflect only an economic reality, society may still be unwilling to accept HCCs that offer different terms for different groups of people.[3] A typical solution would be to force investors to offer the same conditions to everyone. This solution, however, would relieve one group (for example, women) of a higher burden only to place an extra burden on another group (for example, men). In effect, some students would be subsidizing others for reasons that are beyond their control. A fair solution would be to ask society to compensate the under-paid group, rather than shifting the burden to a particular group of people. There are at least two ways of implementing this. First, the state could pay investors the difference between the actual returns obtained from investing in the lower-income group versus the return that would have been obtained had differences in contract terms been allowed. Second, the state could reimburse the lower-income earners the difference between what they actually paid to investors and what they could have paid if they had been part of the privileged group.

The two preceding paragraphs point to an important attribute that HCCs have: they provide transparent information on the inequalities of income between different social groups. We might not like the information revealed, but this is not a good reason for rejecting the instrument. Rather, this information should aid individuals, and society, to make better decisions on how to address these inequalities.

Unfair unlimited upside

A common argument used against the "graduate tax" is that the amount paid by former students has no relation to the amount invested in their education. HCCs *that do not cap students' payments* will face the same charge. Nicholas Barr calls this the Mick Jagger problem: "Mick Jagger was once an accounting student at the London School of Economics. His enormous financial success has no obvious connection with his time at university, yet with a graduate tax he would repay amounts many magnitudes larger than the cost of his studies. As a value judgment, this is unfair."[4]

That value judgment holds as long as the instrument with which education is being financed is considered a loan. However, if the instrument that is financing education is an equity investment, it is not necessarily the case that a relationship has to exist between the amount of the investment and its returns.

In fact, as mentioned earlier, Friedman's original proposal consisted of an instrument that would allow individuals to sell part of their future income:

The device adopted to meet the corresponding problem for other risky investments is equity investment plus limited liability on the part of the shareholders. The counterpart for education would be to "buy" a share in an individual's earning prospects.[5]

Perhaps the reason why the proposal has been almost exclusively linked with a loans system stems from Friedman's own words, for he refers to the providers of capital for this arrangement as "lenders" rather than as "investors."

But HCCs are "equity" investments; they are not loans. The intrinsic or shadow value of the investment will depend on many factors, of which education is only one, and can be very different from the amount that the investor originally gave. Occupation changes are one of the many factors that can affect its value, for better or worse. A lawyer who decides to become a social worker makes the asset worth much less for reasons that have nothing to do with education. An accountant who becomes a pop singer most probably decreases the value of the asset, although some very successful ones will increase its value by several orders of magnitude. These are all possible outcomes and investors and students know it from the moment they sign the HCC. Students are selling an asset, and there is no claim of fairness against what its true value ends up being.

The only claim for fairness would come from having access to relevant information that affects the value of the asset. If there is such information, the claim for fairness comes from the investor who, as explained in chapter 2, has much less information than the student.[6] In particular, students know much better than investors what they plan to do with their careers, and HCCs cannot intervene with these plans. Thus, investors, not students, face a disadvantage when engaging in the contract; they bear the risk of earning low returns, even though they might have a legitimate claim to higher ones.

The defense of a student's free will
Most of the political concerns about HCCs will come from concerns about the relation between students and investors. The concern can be summarized as a fear that investors will exert pressure on students about the path that they should follow once they complete their

education. In other words, there is fear that the system will decay into indentured servitude.

The risk of having pressure from investors on what students do with their lives varies according to the culture where the contracts are struck. Special caution has to be taken where common attitudes point towards this problem. Any hint of abuse on the part of investors can turn a reasonable idea into an oppressive system. Attitudes that are an indication of possible problems are servile relationships between people of different income level, or low regard for the value of freedom.

In addition to the cultural factors, pressure is likely to occur when there is a close relationship between the student and the investor. A close relationship will take place when the performance of the student significantly affects the return to the investor. In circumstances where the investments in students are pooled together, and when investors are able to monitor only the performance of a fund, pressure will be much more difficult to exert.

In contrast with developed economies, developing countries do not have liquid markets that permit the easy creation of impersonal pools of investments, which causes a higher probability of creating close relationships between investors and students with the subsequent risk for students. To prevent this situation, any attempt to create HCCs in developing countries will have to have extra protection for students embedded in its design.

Financial concerns

There are several sources of risk relating to the pay-off on HCCs. The following subsections consider four distinct sources of risk: legal uncertainty, public risk, investment risk, and default. Legal uncertainty stems from the possibility of being unable to enforce HCCs. Public risk relates to uncertainty due to policy changes, and investment risk relates to uncertainty about the behavior, voluntary and involuntary, that students display when they complete their education; while default reflects the possibility that students do not comply with the conditions of the contract.

Legal uncertainty
Because HCCs have yet to be legally tested, there is uncertainty about the legal consequences that signing such a contract would have in the country where they are signed. All investors will be concerned about

(1) the enforceability of the contract, (2) the taxation to which they and students will be subject, and (3) in the case of institutions, the legality of holding such contracts.[7]

The contract is enforceable if the investor can legally demand from the student the percentage of income that the student agreed to pay. If there are particular circumstances in which the contract is not enforceable, then their development will be compromised. For example, according to Roy Chapman, CEO of Human Capital Resources, Inc., there is doubt about whether HCCs would be enforceable in twelve states of the United States or about whether they would be enforceable if the student declared herself bankrupt, and as a consequence Chapman did not proceed with his plans to implement HCCs in the USA. Lawyers consulted in Colombia by the author have raised a similar concern, regarding the possibility that a court could rule the contract invalid on the grounds of the "universal right to education" that every individual has. Further, lawyers consulted by the author in Chile have questioned whether a judge would enforce the payments if these were disproportionately higher than the amount provided by the investor. Presumably, similar objections will arise throughout the world.

In fact, as long as HCCs are viewed through the prism of loans, the potentially high payments that a student would have to make raise concerns about usury and perhaps even of justice, and immediately produce concerns about enforceability. And the prism of viewing student financing as loans is a strong one; Friedman could not avoid it, as his "investment" idea evolved towards a loan (chapter 4).

Another important source of uncertainty is the tax treatment that payments from students will receive. The uncertainty stems from the uniqueness of HCCs and the tendency of viewing them as a loan. Will tax authorities consider payments as interest payments or simply as income from an investment? In some countries (such as Chile, for example) interest payments are subject to value added taxes. Therefore, the value for students, and investors can change significantly, depending on what the official interpretation of the tax authorities is.

As an example, consider what would happen if HCCs were considered as a student "selling" part of her future income. Since the student receives money and forgoes a part of her future income, she should be taxed for the money she receives from the investor, but not over that part of income that is no longer hers. If tax rates were constant, from the point of view of the state there would be no significant difference (in value, though significant in timing).

As an example, John receives $25,000 to finance his education in exchange for 5 percent of his income for the next fifteen years. When he graduates, he joins a company and receives a yearly income of $50,000. According to the terms of the HCC he engaged in, John would have to pay $2,500. Because the $2,500 technically does not belong to him, John's gross income should be $47,500. Accordingly, he should pay taxes on $47,500 and not on $50,000. The extra taxes that John would have to pay when his income is considered to be $50,000 rather than $47,500 makes his investment in education more expensive, and thus, less attractive. Therefore, the student, and indirectly the investor, have an important stake in the taxation of HCCs.[8]

A third concern for the investor, in the particular case of institutions, is whether they are allowed to sign such a contract or not. This is relevant because an important source of the capital for creating HCCs will presumably come from investment funds. These funds, however, are usually regulated as to the type of instruments they can hold. Therefore, if there was uncertainty about how these contracts would be categorized, and whether they could be held by investment institutions, they would probably not invest at all.

The strong case to be made for HCCs will stimulate changes in the law to ensure that the contract is enforceable, that tax payments are fair, and that institutional investors can invest in them. The pressure would be of the same nature that pushed some countries to experiment with vouchers and with charter schools, two options for providing education that will probably not fade away. Still, as long as the legislative power of the country where the HCC will be signed does not pronounce on the subject, or a court rules in one direction or the other, some uncertainty will exist.

Public risk
The enforceability of HCCs is the most important concern for an investor. If there is a high risk that a court might declare HCCs null, such contracts will not exist. In countries that do not have a stable legal system, investors will need extra protection against changes in the regulatory environment.

A way to address enforceability problems in the implementation of HCCs around the world is to have governments assume financial responsibility for the impact that political decisions will have on returns to investors. In other words, government must assume policy risk – it is only fair to place the burden of risk on those who can control it. Doing so might be the only way to ensure that HCCs can exist. Any country with no "sanctity of contract" is too risky to support a market for HCCs without government support.

Once enforceability is no longer a problem investors should evaluate other regulatory issues. The most important of these is the tax treatment of the instrument. The treatment that tax authorities apply to investments in and payments to HCCs will impact the pay-off of both investors and students. From the point of view of investors, tax authorities should provide guidelines on how to treat profits from HCCs.[9] From the point of view of the student, tax authorities should state whether or not HCC payments are tax deductible or not. A tax treatment that would most benefit the development of HCCs is one that would allow investors to depreciate their investment and students to deduct their payments from their income.[10]

Investment risk

If HCCs are enforceable, and their tax treatment clear, investors are left only with the risks directly related to the investment. Risk takes several forms in an HCC. The main ones are: (1) uncertainty about income growth, (2) uncertainty about future occupation, and (3) default risk. These factors will determine the discount rate at which investors value the contracts. In the light of the relatively long-term cash flows of this proposal, small variations in the estimated appropriate discount rate will result in large differences in value. Thus, determining and managing risk will be an important factor for the success of this instrument.

The calculation of the first source of risk is completely independent of students' behavior and can be estimated in the same way as other instruments that rely on the average real growth of income. Investors have no way of influencing the behavior of this variable and their discount rate will depend on how certain they are about their estimates.

The second source of risk is similar to the risk of real income growth with an additional component: a change in the behavior students exhibit towards risk in light of the greater flexibility they have with HCCs as opposed to "mortgage-type" debts. The massive use of HCCs could change the behavior of young graduates who, having no fixed obligation, would be willing to take more risk at the beginning of their

careers.[11] Their behavior would be different from what has histori-
cally been exhibited by students with mortgage-type debts; as such,
their income would be difficult to predict. There is a case for believing
that such a change would *increase* the returns investors obtain.

Accurate predictions of risk from income growth and student behavior will form the basis of successful investment in HCCs. As long as the
returns of education are higher than those on equally risky businesses
there is an opportunity for HCCs to exist.[12]

Default

The third source of risk, default, is not directly related to the business
of education, but to the collection of payments. Given the importance
of this source of risk, it will be explained separately.

The protection that investors feel they have against default will be
the main determinant of the success of HCCs. Default creates a leak
to the high returns that can be obtained from investments in education.
If the leak is too large or difficult to quantify, the opportunity for
investment can vanish. However, with the proper legal environment or
the support of government, this variable can be brought to acceptable
levels.

For the analysis that follows, it is convenient to divide the reasons for
default into two groups: (1) those related to the unwillingness of the individual to repay, and (2) those related to financial distress. This separation is convenient because HCCs are concerned only with the first type
of default. Default related to financial distress disappears because these
contracts will never create an overwhelming burden on individuals.
This is, of course, one of the most important advantages of HCCs.
An appropriate risk analysis should therefore use information from
student loans to estimate the default that is the product of financial distress, and assume that it will not exist, or be greatly reduced, in HCCs.[13]

With regard to unwillingness of students to repay their obligations,
two components should be considered. The first is the default from
students who will simply not make the payments. The second is the
default in the form of hidden or postponed income. Default of the first
kind should be comparable to the rate of individuals defaulting on
debt in the absence of financial distress, thus making this source of risk
quantifiable. Also, the experience with student loans and the success
with which default rates have been managed during the 1990s should

give confidence to investors about the possibility of bringing default to other consumer debt levels.[14]

The aspect of HCCs that is likely to raise the most concern among investors is the incentive that students have to postpone or hide their income. Postponing income can be done in so many different ways that no contract will be able to cover them all. Thus, the contract should explicitly state that any income derived from the student's productive efforts during the repayment period should be considered income for the purposes of determining the student's repayment obligations.

This source of risk is considerably higher in developing countries. A nationwide student loan program is probably available in just a few places, thus history about the behavior of students towards debt is scarce. Moreover, the lack of widely used financial services diminishes the importance that individuals give to having a "clean" credit history. Also, there will probably be additional obstacles in determining a student's income. However, these obstacles in developing countries are not insurmountable. Chapter 10 explicitly offers alternatives for managing these risks.

The possibility of individuals hiding their income to reduce their payments (and possibly their taxes) is a threat to the functioning of the system and should be an important source of attention for the success of HCCs. The main defense that investors will have is the alignment of their interests with those of the tax-collecting agency. As with the default of payments, countries with an effective income tax system have a great advantage over other countries since students' incomes are much easier to determine. A student who chooses to hide income faces prosecution from the government, thereby raising the cost of using such a strategy.

In the particular case of HCCs with a cap on the payments an individual will make in any given year, investors can address the hidden income by always invoicing a student for the amount of the cap in the contract, and including a clause in the contract that places a burden upon the student to present acceptable evidence of their income if they desire to pay an amount lower than what is suggested by the cap.[15] Under this arrangement, investors need worry only about the fraction of students whose payments do not reach the specified cap. This alternative is not perfect, though, because students will always be a step ahead of investors when it comes to finding ways to under-state their income.

There is a final concern regarding default that has to do with students' high mobility. One of the reasons banks do not like to offer loans to students is the ease with which they can move around and, thus, default on their payments. When students reside outside the country where the HCC was signed, they will be extremely difficult to track. Investors will need to rely either on the student's goodwill, or on a legal arrangement between the country where the student lives and where the contract was signed, or on a mechanism that engages a third party, such as the student's parents, in the contract between the student and the investor.

Emigration can be particularly relevant in countries where those who emigrate tend to do it permanently, rather than temporarily. For instance, US citizens who emigrate usually do so with the hope of returning to their country at some moment in the future. In countries like the USA, therefore, emigration will not be an important concern.[16] In contrast, foreigners who seek to immigrate to the USA are usually looking forward to creating a new life for themselves and their families in the long term. In this case, different arrangements should be sought to ensure that individuals continue with their payments.

Nicholas Barr addresses the same problem when he speaks of collection mechanisms for income-contingent loans (ICLs). His ideas on this point can be applied entirely to HCCs, since the issue is literally equivalent.[17]

First, he points out that the main problem with emigration takes place when the address of the individual is not known. When the address is known, he states, individuals usually comply. Only when they do not does the loan end up being in default. Thus, the main task for addressing labor mobility is to find efficient ways to track the addresses of individuals.

A basic proposal for solving this problem is to ask the tax authorities of other countries to exchange information about immigrants from a particular nation. As Barr states, making progress in this area should not be as difficult as initially thought, given that tax authorities already have an immigrant's details and that this kind of collaboration already exists within the European Union. Further, because emigration is mostly from poor countries to rich ones, any developing country could deal with the vast majority of their student loans simply by dealing with the tax authorities of the OECD countries. The role of the foreign tax agencies remains *only* to provide the basic information.

A more radical approach proposed by Barr, certainly a visionary one, consists of tax authorities of all countries collecting student loan repayments. In his own words:

With such an arrangement, loan repayments are transparent with respect to international boundaries. Students are free to migrate, with benefits both for labor mobility and individual freedom. The arrangement also makes it possible to have a loan scheme in developing countries, from which many of the best-educated people emigrate. There are further developmental advantages. It would be possible for the EU or the World Bank to establish an International Learning Bank from which students from poor countries would borrow to finance their tertiary education – both those who subsequently stay at home and those who emigrate.[18]

For implementation purposes, the first step is to follow the first recommendation, i.e., information-sharing. Once information-sharing is in place and running, the second approach can be implemented, even if only partially.

These arrangements have to be pursued aggressively since in the absence of default resulting from emigration, investors in some countries will probably be better off if students emigrate. This is probably the case between emigration between developing countries and industrialized nations. HCCs would actually compensate the "brain drain" that many countries suffer by sending back to the country where the contract was struck part of the extra income that in many cases motivates emigration.

Clearing the hurdles

The last sections showed three main hurdles in implementing HCCs today: (1) protection for the student, (2) protection for the investor, and (3) collection of payments.

The first problem is easily addressed in the design of the contract. There might be some countries where special emphasis from the government might be required to ensure that investors do not interfere with the student's decisions. This should not be a problem if HCCs are part of a government's effort to reform financing for higher education.

The second hurdle may not be much of a problem in developed countries, where laws are stable. For instance, MyRichUncle™ has already started offering HCCs in the USA. In the case of developing countries, investors will probably demand governments to assume the "policy" risk. As with the protection for students, this is feasible if the implementation of HCCs is part of an education-financing reform led by government. Governments can assume policy risk by explicitly agreeing to compensate investors for changes in the amount they can collect due to government's decisions.

The third hurdle is the one that demands most attention. To overcome it, HCCs can look to the experience of other policy proposals that have successfully used governments' tax collection agencies to collect payments.

Two examples are prominent: first, the implementation of private pension funds and, second, several ICL programs that use the tax collection agencies to collect loan payments. The experiences pioneered by Chile with private pension funds, and by Australia with ICLs, are examples of policy programs that use the tax system to reduce collection costs for programs that are not directly related to taxes. The concept applicable to HCCs is that the state can successfully institutionalize the enforcement of payments to entities other than itself.[19] The resulting collection costs are very low[20] and make the investment in education more attractive. Chapter 10 explores this idea more deeply.

Conclusion

All the important objections regarding HCCs can be addressed. From an ethical standpoint, as long as the student is protected against any kind of abuse on the part of investors, there should not be any concern about the contract being comparable to indentured servitude. There is no bondage between the investor and the student, and the latter gains access to new options of which the investor is one of the main enablers. From a financial perspective, the high returns of education compared with other investments of similar risk show that there is an opportunity for investing in education where the investor can obtain an average return higher than his cost of borrowing.[21] The question that then remains is whether the difference is enough to support the administrative costs and the defaults on payments. Defaults can be brought to acceptable levels by using some of the lessons from the history of student loans in the USA and by asking government to shape the legal institutions needed to increase the likelihood that students fulfill their obligations.

Because the costs that do not depend directly on the economics of education can be so high as to destroy the profitability of investors, the role of public policy for the implementation of HCCs is extremely important, particularly in countries where sanctity of contract does not exist. Investors need to know that institutions will support their legitimate claims to part of an individual's income, or at least will take responsibility for not supporting them. Possible alternatives for achieving that objective are discussed in chapter 10.

9 | *Lessons from the implementation of income-contingent loans*

T HE years since 1970 have seen several attempts to introduce income-contingent schemes (ICLs) in the financing of education, and several such schemes have now been implemented successfully in different countries. As we saw in chapter 4, ICLs are loans in which students pay a percentage of their income until they repay the loan and accrued interest, or until a maximum repayment period has been reached. They differ from human capital contracts (HCCs), as in an HCC students pay for a fixed period of time, regardless of the amount repaid. In chapter 6, we discussed how ICLs were an income-contingent repayment mechanism and therefore offered some of the same advantages of HCCs. We also discussed in that chapter how HCCs displayed some additional attributes that ICLs did not have. Chapter 7 was devoted to showing the relationship between HCCs and ICLs through the introduction of human capital options (HCOs). Now we shall look for lessons in the implementation of ICLs that can be used to improve the possibilities of success in implementing HCCs.

This chapter will look in detail at the program Yale started in 1971 and at that implemented in Australia in 1989. In addition, a brief description is provided of other income-contingent programs. The lessons that can be drawn from these two cases are relevant for HCCs because ICLs and HCCs share the income-contingent feature. This is one of the most important features of HCCs, so the implementation of HCCs will probably face similar challenges to those ICLs have faced since the 1970s.

The Yale experiment[1]

In 1971, Yale University started a program (the Tuition Postponement Program, or TPP) that included income-contingent payments. The program was devised as an alternative for students who were seeing their financing opportunities shrinking as government cut the amount offered in loans and grants. The experiment was designed originally to last until 1976, but then was extended one further year. Students who joined the university in 1976 or before were allowed to continue in it until graduation. Thus, financing actually lasted several more years. After this period the program stopped, as new funds were available from other sources and as Yale felt the need of additional help from public agencies to finance deferred payments. More than two decades after the program started it was still collecting payments from students who were involved in it in 2001. The negative opinion that some of them have expressed regarding it has attracted some public attention, and is one of the reasons why the case is discussed here.

Description of the program[2]

The program had two distinct features that made it different from other financing schemes available at the time. First, payments would be income-contingent. Second, individual loans would be grouped to form "group loans," creating mutual responsibility among classmates to repay their obligation.[3]

The first feature stated that students would repay each year 0.0004 percent of their annual income for each dollar received. Each year, a student's debt would be calculated as the difference between the value of the loan plus the accrued interest to date and the value of the payments and their accrued interest to date. The interest rate was agreed to be variable, reflecting Yale's own cost of capital and the administrative costs of the program, though there was a cap at 12 percent or at 1 percent above the University's cost of capital. Each year, the University would determine the interest rate for the loan for the next year.

The second feature, and the more controversial one, grouped each individual's loan into a cohort. Under this arrangement the debts and interest accrued by *all* the students in a given cohort were summed together as well as the payments (calculated as explained in the previous paragraph) and their accrued interest. The difference between the debts and payments, including their respective accrued interest, was the balance that the cohort owed to the university. Every student in the cohort would have to continue making income-contingent payments until the balance of the *cohort* was zero. The group was responsible even for the payments of those students who defaulted on their loan.

This second feature redistributed the payments that students of a given cohort had to make. High-income earners would end up paying more, in both absolute and present value terms, than low-income earners. The redistribution took place only between students of the same cohort. Thus, cohorts of above-average income earners and others with lower-than-average income earners would not redistribute among themselves. However, because the University created the cohorts randomly, there is no particular reason to think that there would be significant differences between them.

The redistribution was not unlimited. The contract included the condition that an individual's obligations would finish when the University had received 150 percent of the debt and accrued interest from her. Thus, the responsibility of a given individual towards a group was capped at 50 percent above her own responsibility. This condition was offered as a "buyout" to individuals who didn't wish to continue in the program.

The last important feature was that the obligation of the cohort would not last more than thirty-five years. It was expected that most cohorts would complete their obligations in a much shorter period, and indeed several ones did finish before that.

Under the program, students with high incomes would end up paying more than they would have otherwise paid had they taken out a normal loan. On the other hand, low-income students would pay less than they would have otherwise had to pay. The spirit of the program was to create such redistribution between high-income and low-income earners, to relieve low-income earners from financial distress and from a poor return on their education.

Yale's income-contingent repayment plan results

As publicized in *The Wall Street Journal*,[4] not everything went as smoothly as planned. The two main problems were related to each other: negative public opinion and high default rates. Additionally, a change in the law in 1986 created a significant impact on the attractiveness of the project to students who were still paying, making both public opinion and default rates worse.

Yale faced default rates of 15 percent, way above their original expectations. Education loans have typically had high default rates. But, given Yale's arrangement, their impact on the project was much more dramatic. When a student defaults, the obligations of all the other students in the cohort increase. After a few cases, members of the cohort started to feel that they were unfairly carrying the burden of classmates' debts. This, in turn, increased the chances that an individual would default. Since there was no effective way of creating "group pressure" on those who had not paid, this cycle deteriorated as time passed. Additionally, since Yale was a university and not a bank, it did not have the knowledge or the resources for collecting debt effectively. This made it even harder, or more expensive, for the University to stop the drain from defaults.

The low morale of individuals who were still paying, coupled with the long-term nature of the loan, increased the feeling of frustration and inequity. Because the interest rate was variable, set to meet Yale's cost of capital, and interest rates rose considerably at the beginning of the 1980s, the nominal value of the debt grew considerably. Even though the net present value (NPV) of the loan was the same as before, there was a negative psychological effect in seeing the debt rise in value.

Until 1986, the fact that the interest payments by students were tax deductible made the cost of the loan cheaper for everybody who was enrolled in the program. However, that year a legal change made it no longer possible for individuals to deduct their interest from their taxes. As a result, the cost of the debt increased significantly for them. Many decided to finish their obligation by paying the amount needed to cover the 150 percent of their loan and accrued interest. Those who remained in the program, though, were penalized with the extra cost.

Yale had effectively to modify the original plan to cope with the growing pressure of dissatisfied alumni. These modifications ended up forgiving part of the remaining balance of cohorts who would have had to continue paying for additional years, bringing an end to the problem in 2001. In spite of these problems, the program offers valuable lessons for the implementation of HCCs. These are discussed below.

Lessons from Yale

The main lessons from Yale's experiment, after more than two decades, relate to (1) the time frame of the program, (2) perception of the time-value of money, (3) the redistributive nature of the loan, and (4) the collection agency employed. These are discussed below.

First, having thirty-five years as the maximum repayment period created the feeling of "perpetual obligation" in the students who were still paying their loans. The long-term repayment period is not necessarily negative; it actually corresponds to the long-term benefits of having additional education. So the fact that it is seen as burdensome attests to the students' paradigm of how long a given obligation should be. Acknowledging that periods of time comparable with the productive life of an individual are going to generate negative feelings is extremely important for the implementation of future similar programs. Either the period should be shortened or steps taken to change the paradigm of how long a legitimate obligation should last.

Shorter periods of time have a disadvantage. The profits from education come during the whole productive life of the individual, and trying to repay education costs in a shorter period creates a higher-than-needed financial burden during the repayment years and no burden at all during the rest of the productive life. This imbalance can threaten the existence of the program. In the case of ICLs, the burden would translate into higher percentages of income dedicated to the repayment of the loan.

Changing the paradigm on how long a legitimate obligation should last can also be difficult. However, because it makes more financial sense to have repayment periods last as long as the individual's productive life, this should be attempted first, rather than shortening the repayment period. One possible way to change it is by pointing at the facts that taxes last as long as there is income, and that other obligations with similar long-term implications should be considered *as burdensome or less* than taxes. Whereas it is true that there is no consensus on the amount of "fair" taxes, there seems to be public tolerance for the fact that they are for life. In other words, the public considers it legitimate to have taxes for long periods of time. The public also seems to consider it legitimate to pay thirty-year mortgages, although this might be aided by the fact that they can finish their contract by selling their property, something they cannot do with their education. Therefore, there are reasons to suppose that the public can eventually see as legitimate, and desirable, long-term repayment periods for their education loans.[5] The negative reaction against long repayment periods should warn investors of the time frame they are going to offer their students for repayment. To improve the amount of funding that each student can receive, longer repayment periods will be required. Thus, the implementation of HCCs will require an effort to change the current paradigm to a new one that accepts that the long-term benefits of education can be coupled with long-term obligations.[6] As

an alternative, smaller funds can be made available and a shorter repayment period can be used. On this matter, however, there is still
information to be generated from Australia's program, given that, as
discussed in the next section, it was implemented only in 1989.

Second, the interest rate that was charged on the loans, which represents the time value of money, also generated a problem. The compounding interest over a long period of time created a relevant increase
in the *nominal amount* that an individual would end up paying. Even if
the interest rate were set at the risk-adjusted rate for the loan, in which
case the NPV of the payments equals the value of the loan, there was a
psychological effect from the nominal amount paid. The reaction was
a negative feeling of inequity, paying many times the actual worth of
something.[7] This feeling triggered negative public opinion and created
a justification in a student's mind for defaulting.

An alternative for solving this problem has been to have a zero real
interest rate, or to implement a mechanism for creating an implicit interest rate. However, having the real interest rate below the risk-adjusted
one is not optimal and some one has to pay for the low risk-adjusted
returns obtained from such a loan.[8] The efficient amount of resources
will be allocated only when the proper interest rate is recognized by investors. For this reason, having an artificially low interest rate is not an
optimal solution. It can solve the problem of negative public opinion
at the expense of fewer resources for financing education. The alternative of creating an implicit interest rate can partially solve the problem.
One way of doing this is to offer a discount for upfront payments.
The solution is still not ideal because the implicit interest rate will vary
inversely with the repayment period and thus it is unlikely that it will
match the risk-adjusted one.[9]

The remaining alternative has to do with changing the perception of
nominal value as the real value of something. Education on the time-
value of money can be an important aid in changing the perception
of unfairness. If students understand that the resources they are using
have value in time, and that they should also pay for that value, then
the negative feeling against the amount of nominal payments would
decrease. Although it might be unrealistic to expect such an attitude
change in the short or medium term, efforts to educate the beneficiaries
of loans should be employed constantly in an effort to create long-
term attitude change. For the particular case of countries experiencing
high inflation, the use of a constant purchasing power currency to

calculate the payments made can decrease the perception of making large payments based on the original nominal amount. Countries with a history of hyperinflation are used to these currencies and these should be used.

Although HCCs do not have an interest rate as part of the contract, they might face a similar problem if economically successful students complain about the value of the payments they are making. Obtaining high payments from the high-income earners is part of the essence of an HCC if the investor is going to share the upside as well as the downside of a student's income potential. There is no reason for expecting that the negative reaction that Yale faced would not also happen with HCCs. High-income individuals engaged in this kind of contract will probably react by arguing that they are over-paying for the education they received.[10] The case, however, is not as strong as with ICLs, because the ones who would be complaining would be those who did better than average, while in ICLs those who pay for long periods are those who have relatively low incomes. Likewise, public emphasis should be placed on the fact that the investor is taking the risk with the student, and that more than a fixed payment, an HCC is a partnership on education.

The third lesson offered by Yale's experiment is the growing perception of inequity in the redistribution of payments made by individuals of a given cohort. Even though originally students viewed positively that high-income students would pay more than low-income earners, after some years of actual payments, discontent from "subsidizing" others grew and contributed to the negative public opinion of the program. The problem increased with the fact that those still paying were subsidizing those who defaulted. To illustrate this point, consider a group with ten students. After the first student defaults on her loan, each individual's obligations increase by one-tenth. The burden has increased, and other students who were close to defaulting will now do so. After the second, third and fourth students have defaulted on their loans, the six remaining individuals will have obligations almost twice as high as they originally had. This example shows how defaulting individuals will tend to increase, destroying the whole system. The original "group responsibility" was weakened by the fact that there was no way of enforcing the responsibility of the members in the group.[11]

The existence of a cap on the total amount that a student has to pay during the life of the loan decreases the redistribution of payments between students of the same cohort, and thus can counteract the negative feeling that paying for others creates in some high-income individuals. From Yale's experience, it is clear that a 50 percent premium is still seen as too high. Only experience will show what the proper level is.

From the previous discussion, it can be concluded that the implementation of other income-contingent repayment schemes (ICRS) should avoid the concept of group responsibility when the group cannot effectively exert pressure on the individual. HCCs do not have this problem, because even though on average the investor expects to compensate for losses generated by low-income earners with the gains obtained from high-income earners, *the behavior of the group does not affect the payments that an individual has to make.*

Finally, Yale also showed that it lacked the competency to collect payments from students who were in default. This stems from the fact that Yale's competencies were in teaching and research, and that financial institutions were the ones with expertise in collecting payments. Efficient financing arrangements should try to let each institution do what it does best.

This lesson applies to any kind of student financing system. For the particular case of HCCs, the efficient collection of payments will be a key component for their success as a funding option for students. Collection might be better left to banks and other payment collection agencies.

It is tempting to agree with some alumni and the writer of *The Wall Street Journal* article that Yale's experiment was a failure. However, given the example that it provided for the implementation of other income-contingent repayment mechanisms, it should better be considered as a pioneering program learning from experience. Furthermore, because the program was a combination of income-contingent payments and a "group redistribution" scheme, the program permits us to study the effects of effectively translating part of the risk of the investment to the group or cohort. As discussed in chapter 7, one of the advantages of viewing ICLs as a combination of loans and HCOs is that risk can be separated and attributed to other parties, rather than forcing other members of the cohort to take it on. Even though it was not an acclaimed success, the learning gained from creating a better system for financing access to higher education cannot be overlooked. Yale's program stands as a unique experience and thus is a benchmark for further developments.

HCCs should not have the negative public opinion that Yale's program had because the contract with the student has several differences. As mentioned above, an individual is responsible for her own income, unaffected by the performance of others and only those who do well pay more than what they received. Therefore, perceptions of inequity because of paying for others should not exist in this case and making long "enslaving" payments is less likely.

Now we turn our attention to a program that was a pioneer in its implementation, using a public collecting agency to enforce income-contingent payments; this is Australia's Higher-Education Contribution Scheme (HECS) program. This is the case of a public lender and collector whereas Yale is the case of a private lender and collector. This difference will offer a further perspective on the results that can be achieved with income-contingent arrangements.

Australia's Higher-Education Contribution Scheme program[12]

The Higher-Education Contribution Scheme (HECS) was a radical new policy for Australia's government. The system consisted of a unique ICRS for higher-education students. Because it took an opposite direction from what had been the government's policy towards public education, the example of HECS implementation offers an excellent case study for the possible implementation of HCCs. The following discussion outlines the events that led to the implementation of HECS in 1989, and describes the scheme as it was then. Since then, there have been several modifications to the program, particularly concerning how much is charged to students in different fields of study and what percentage of income is collected as a function of total income. None of these changes modifies the essence of the program: income-contingent loan payments collected by the state.

Background[13]

To understand the implementation of Australia's HECS program, we should understand the policies that drove its higher-education system to the necessity of a new model for financing its higher education.

Australia' higher-education sector is mainly provided by the state. Therefore, the state decides how much to charge for attending, and all students are subject to these fees. Prior to 1974, those fees represented around 25 percent of total cost, with the remaining 75 percent subsidized by the state. However, in 1974 government abolished all fees on higher education, leaving all the burden of education costs on the state. During the next decade, at least three factors caused the government to rethink its position: first, increasing demand; second, an increasingly negative public view of state-financed higher education; and third, the tide of liberalization that questioned the rationale for government spending in several areas, including education.

The first factor was a pragmatic one: as the demand for higher education rose, the government faced higher budget outlays to finance education. The increased retention in high-school rates made it clear that there would be a continuous increase in the demand for university places, thus increasing the budget needs for higher education. This pressure threatened to make the current system unsustainable.

The second factor related to the emergence of the view that higher-education financing through tax revenue was extremely regressive. The system is regressive because only a fraction of the population attends higher-education institutions, and those who attend are also the ones who enjoy higher incomes thereafter. Thus, public financing of higher education obtained the resources from everyone, including the majority who did not enjoy the benefits of higher education, and invested them in those who would enjoy higher average incomes. The justice of this system was debatable, and public attention was being drawn towards this point.

The third factor that contributed to the policy change was the growing skepticism towards government spending. After some countries such as the UK and Chile, pioneered economywide privatization programs, the privatization wave grew stronger in many other parts of the world. Skeptics questioned the role of governments in the financing and operation of many activities, and higher education was one of them.

Those three factors triggered change in Australia's policy of free higher education, implying that fees would be charged. However, that change brought with it the challenge with which this book is concerned: how can universities charge fees without affecting the possibility of low-income students attending higher education? There was a clear goal not to erect a financial barrier against economically disadvantaged students.

Chapter 2 explains why there is an inefficient borrowing market for financing education. The two main reasons are lack of collateral and high collection costs for financial institutions. In absence of such a market, low-income students will be affected by the decision to charge fees for higher education. Having in mind this limitation, ICLs were studied as a viable alternative for charging fees for higher education without affecting low-income students. Because of their nature, ICLs do not pose a financial burden for the student, and thus allows her to have a financial obligation without the risk of falling into financial distress because of it.

Although several authors had published theoretical work on the idea, it had never been brought into practice on a countrywide scale. Therefore, those bringing forward the idea within the Wran committee faced considerable resistance from several political quarters, including the Labor Party, because of the lack of precedent. First, some of them raised questions of whether it would work or not, and whether it would actually help those that it intended to help, the economically disadvantaged students. Second, the tax collection agency opposed it on grounds that its work was not to collect debts. Third, it did not solve the immediate funding needs of the state.

The first concern reflects the typical reaction to anything that is new. Without any example of a working model, the risk of implementing a revolutionary policy seems high. Resistance to change is a common barrier any new idea has to face. The evidence after some fourteen years of implementation has suggested that their concerns were unjustified. This evidence is studied later in the chapter.

The second concern probably reflects the tax collection bureaucracy's resistance to change. The supporters of HECS had to find evidence that the tax office did engage in the collection of debts to prove that they might as well collect higher-education debts. The example used was the case when individuals who had to give family support had their contribution deducted from their paycheck, which was also known as the "non-custodial parent contribution."

The third concern potentially exists in every case in which the introduction of ICLs is being considered.[14] To solve the problem, the possibility of making upfront payments was included in the proposal (see Wran, 1988; Edwards, Howard and Miller, 2002). Offering a discount on upfront payments naturally creates an incentive for those who can to pay upon enrollment instead of taking a loan.

Another important characteristic that the program had was to establish that the payments from ex-students would be used exclusively to finance higher education via a trust fund.[15] This condition was included to avoid the use of the funds for other functions, affecting the general budget. In effect, this measure tried to keep payments from loans independent from a "graduate" tax, which would be subject to political pressure and instability, and also probably be questioned on grounds of earmarking tax revenues.

Once the government made the decision to go ahead with the idea, the next stage addressed the details of how the program would operate. The basic characteristics to be determined were the fees to be charged and the repayment schedule as a function of income. The loan would be offered to any student who was accepted in a university.

Program implementation

To implement the initial program in 1989, two important questions had to be answered: (1) how much should be charged to each student, and (2) should different amounts be charged to different students? The framework used to answer these questions is discussed below.

Theoretically, the optimal fee for higher education should be less than 100 percent of the cost. This follows from the positive "neighborhood" effects[16] that society perceives from the higher education of its citizens. By giving a subsidy, the individual is compensated for the benefits she gives society for which she cannot charge. Moreover, economic theory predicts that if the "neighborhood" effect is not corrected, the optimal amount of investment will not be achieved. However, the "neighborhood" effects from higher education are highly qualitative and difficult to quantify, and because of this there is little guidance on their magnitude. The subsidy should not cover 100 percent of the cost because in spite of the "neighborhood" effects there is still a private benefit in the form of a higher post-education income. Thus, there should be a fee, but it should be below the full cost of education.

Another issue when determining the fee to charge is whether or not to charge different fees for different careers. In theory, because the cost of different careers varies, the fee for each career should be different. For example, Bruce Chapman (1997) says that the average cost of medicine is about five times the cost of law, accounting, and general arts subjects.[17]

Table 9.1 *Percentage of income required by HECS, 1996*

Taxable income ($A)[a]	Annual repayment rate (%)
0–27,674	0
27,675–31,449	3
31,450–44,029	4
44,030 or more	5

Note:
[a] The exchange rate in 1996 fluctuated around $A1.30 per US$1.

The way in which the two issues – what the fee should be and whether or not it should vary by career – were solved was by a search for simplicity. The fee to be charged would be around 20–25 percent of the average full-time higher-education cost per student. The determination of this number was arbitrary, based on the precedent of fees charged before they were abolished in 1974. Under the premise of keeping the HECS program simple, the fee for different careers was kept constant.

There are two important factors that remained to be determined: first, the interest rate; and, second, the repayment schedule. The real interest rate for the loans was set at zero, varying the nominal rate with inflation. The fact that the interest rate is set below a market value, even below the risk-free rate, has consequences that will be described later in this chapter. The reason for arguing in favor of keeping the real interest rate at zero is that this prevents an accumulation of debt similar to what happened to Yale's students.[18] The repayment schedule in 1996 values was as shown in table 9.1.

The percentages were fixed at an amount that would not place an excessive burden on the student, and that would permit the repayment of the debt before the student's retirement. They were progressive so as to accelerate the repayment of high-income earners and were equal to zero below a certain threshold so as not to place a burden on low-income earners. Payments would last as long as the student had income and had a balance on the loan and accrued interest. As will be discussed later, accelerating the repayment of high-income earners in a context where the interest rate is below the risk-adjusted one increases the NPV of the payments made by high-income earners.

Since part of the motivation for the HECS program was to deal with a budget issue, the Australian government still had the incentive to charge fees upfront. To create an incentive for students to pay upon enrollment the program offered them a 25 percent reduction in the nominal value of the debt if they paid the fee upfront.

HECS results

In 1996, the fee charged for any career was $A2,442 (around US$1,900), for a full-time year of higher-education study, with pro rata charges for part-time students. This amount covered 23 percent of the total education expenses for the state. Most students preferred to defer their payments rather than paying upon enrollment.

HECS produced more than $A1.6 billion in additional revenue for the Australian government from their introduction in 1989 until 1996. The payments represented around 10 percent of the outlays for education and it was expected to increase in the future. The studies conducted by Harding (1993, 1995)[19] conservatively estimate that 96 and 77 percent of the male and female HECS debts, respectively, would be paid by the time graduates were sixty-five years old. Chapman and Nicholls (2003) state that administration costs have been around 0.5 percent percent of total HECS revenue, a percentage that can be considered very small considering the efforts that must be performed to collect payments. Thus, HECS did achieve one of its goals: to create additional revenues for financing education.

Evidence suggests that HECS has also achieved a second goal of charging a fee without erecting a barrier for low-income students. Government outlays have increased, in part financed by HECS, achieving an average 4 percent yearly growth in the number of higher-education students. Of most importance for studying the viability of HECS, the increase has been evenly distributed for students of different income level. Bruce Chapman (1997) includes the graph in figure 9.1 to make this point. Each bar in the graph represents the proportion of 18-year-olds enrolled in education in 1988 and 1993.

The increase in enrollment of students from high- and low-wealth families increased by 33 and 31 percent, respectively. Moreover, in a survey conducted by researchers from Curtin and Flinders Universities, the researchers found that, in general, HECS was not an important factor for a student not choosing to enroll. In another survey performed by Ernst and Young, HECS ranked 13 out of 17 factors that might contribute to affect the decision of a final-year high-school student

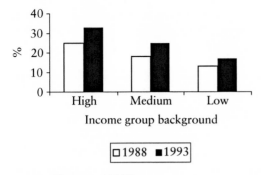

Source: Chapman (1997).

Figure 9.1 Participation of different social groups in the Australian higher-education system

whether or not to continue with higher education. Thus, given that student enrollments from different social grounds increased in the same proportion, and that HECS seems to not be an important factor affecting the decision whether or not to continue with higher education, this evidence suggests that HECS has not affected the probabilities of enrollment for a low-income student. In other words, HECS has charged students without marginalizing a particular income group.

The cost for students

Two features of the income-contingent program used in Australia merit additional discussion: first, the interest rate; and, second, the discount received for upfront payments upon enrollment.

Consider first the interest rate. Because the interest rate is below the rate that reflects the risk of the loan, students who pay slowly receive a larger subsidy than those who repay fast. Students with high incomes will pay faster and pay a greater amount in present value terms. Students with low incomes will pay slower and pay less. Thus, the present value of the debt will be different for each individual. However, both high- and low-income earners pay a sum less in value than the one originally given to them. Thus, both are subsidized, with low-income earners receiving a higher subsidy.[20] This would not happen if the interest rate reflected the risk of the loan. In that case the value of the debt would be the same for everyone, regardless of the time taken to pay it back.

The desirability of such a subsidy is questionable. Certainly, having an interest rate higher than the risk-adjusted rate would punish low-income earners and would hardly be defensible. However, the case for an additional subsidy is not clear, especially if the system is going to be used to attract private investors who would be interested in obtaining a risk-adjusted return.[21]

The second feature that merits discussion is the discount that students who pay upon enrollment obtain in the cost of their tuition. The result is an implied real interest rate on the loan. This "implied" interest rate also differs for each individual, decreasing as the time the student takes to pay back the loan increases.

The net effect of the subsidized interest rate and the implied interest rate resulting from having the option to make a discounted upfront payment depends on the repayment speed of the student. Students with high initial incomes who opt to take the loan might end up paying a higher interest than the risk-adjusted one. Thus, the discount for upfront payments provides an incentive for students of careers with high initial incomes to pay the full cost upon enrollment rather than taking the loan. Low-income careers will probably still pay the equivalent of a subsidized interest rate by paying through HECS.

Lessons from the Australian experiment

HECS has increased government's capacity to provide higher education in a way that does not marginalize incoming students from low-income backgrounds. Thus, the program fulfilled its two main goals and can be described as a success. Its implementation, as well as its performance since 1989, provides valuable lessons for other countries that wish to implement other ICRS, like HCCs.

The first lesson relates to the collection system. The program was successful in part because of the previous existence of a well-developed tax collecting agency that can obtain payments with a low marginal cost. As stated above, a collection cost of 0.5 percent percent is extremely low for collecting loan payments. The success of the program is dependent on having a reliable cost-effective method for collecting payments, and the method used in the Australian case might not be present in other countries. In particular, private entities that do not have an incentive to collect, like a private university, would find it very difficult to replicate the collection success of HECS. Yale is a dramatic example that supports this conclusion.[22]

The desirability of using the state as a collection agency has been tested by the use of HECS. Collecting debts from students is very expensive for private institutions, banking or other non-financial institutions (such as universities). On the one hand, there is no collateral to be liquidated by the bank. On the other hand, the process of taking legal action against an individual is on average very expensive relative to the amount owed. When the state acts as a collecting agency the marginal cost is low, since the collecting mechanism is already in place. Thus, traditional financial institutions can hardly compete with the state in collecting income-contingent payments from education.

These results show that the special features of HECS, income-contingent payments and collection through the tax collecting agency, make a system based on income-contingent payments feasible. Because they increase the capital available for financing education without creating a barrier against low-income students, they should be regarded as an excellent alternative to the traditional solutions for financing education. HCCs can build on these lessons for their own implementation as the effectiveness of the collection agency will be a key factor in the success or failure of the implementation. For instance, the Australian experience shows that a government agency can substitute private efforts in countries where a private enterprise would not be likely to succeed. Furthermore, Australia's case shows that it might be desirable to have the state involved in the collection of payments because it usually possesses the most advanced income-contingent collection mechanism in a country.

Additionally, HECS provides two lessons regarding the *process* of implementing ICLs. First, Edwards, Howard and Miller (2002) describe HECS as a painless method for introducing higher-education charges. This is a key concept for bringing about change in the financing of higher education. Because opposition to change will come from many directions, a system that can be introduced without creating a shock is a powerful policy tool.

Second, HECS also shows that the immediate need for funds can be overcome if an alternative to upfront payments is provided. That was the purpose of the inclusion of an upfront payment (see Wran, 1988; Edwards, Howard and Miller, 2002). The soundness of doing so is reinforced by the conclusions of chapter 7. Because an ICL can be understood as a combination of a traditional loan and an option, the payments that students who take the loan make should include the value of that option. Therefore, students who do not take the loan should not be charged for the value of the loan and should pay less than students who do take the financing.

Other examples of income-contingent loans

Besides Yale's TPP and Australia's HECS program, other examples are worth mentioning as they have particular features not present in the HECS or Yale program. These features can provide other lessons for the implementation of HCCs. New Zealand, Chile, Sweden, and Ghana are discussed below.

New Zealand introduced its ICL program in 1991. The system was quite similar to Australia's HECS program, but included some significant differences. First, with the intention of improving universities' responses to demand from students, New Zealand universities were allowed to vary the amount charged to each student. Second, the interest rate of the loan carried a market interest rate.

In contrast to HECS, New Zealand's program has been criticized widely, forcing the government to modify it in 2000. Criticism forced government to change the interest rate of the loans, bringing it down from a market value to zero while the student remained in the university, and an amount that changed depending on the graduate's employment circumstances. This change is a step away from loans that can be financed using private capital. Furthermore, Chapman and Nicholls (2002) point to the increase in administration costs that tampering with the interest rate will bring. Further changes might come as students press for more advantageous conditions.

New Zealand's ICLs were the ones that most closely resembled a market-based loan. However, because of political instability the mechanism had to be changed. This is a reminder that the most efficient solution from a purely economic perspective may not be politically sustainable. In those cases, leaving the doctrine aside and looking for a flexible implementation alternative might be better than not having a program at all. Chapman and Nicholls (2002) conclude that such flexibility is an indispensable ingredient in the successful design of this kind of instrument.

Chile's University Credit Solidarity Funds (Fondos Solidarios de Crédito Universitario) are funds that use ICLs to finance students. These funds replaced the previous fixed-payment loan system, called University Credit (Crédito Universitario) in 1994 (Leiva, 2002). Even though the payment mechanism changed, the system is still known as University Credit.[23] The loan carries a real interest rate of 2 percent, and requires from the student annual payments of the lesser of 5 percent of income and a fixed amount. Maximum repayment periods are twelve or fifteen years, depending on the amount of the balance due in the twelfth year. The University Credit is made available according to the student's background. Each university is responsible for collecting the payments from the University Credit, resulting in widely varied collection results from institution to institution, with average countrywide cost-recovery levels around 60 percent (Camhi and Latuf, 2000).[24]

The system is not widely considered as successful. First, cost-recovery levels are low (although typical if contrasted with international standards). Second, the amounts available for lending are far from satisfying student demand (Leiva, 2002). To increase the capital available for higher-education financing, the system needs to attract private capital, and it needs to collect payments using different means than those used today. But engaging private lenders will not be easy: the Chilean government attempted to sell its loans to the private sector and faced fierce opposition from students.

Chile's example reinforces the notion that universities are not good debt collectors (as Yale turned out not to be). Universities know how to teach and do research, not how to collect debt. Experience points out to the promotion, when designing a higher-education program, of a separate entity to handle payment collection.

Ghana implemented an income-contingent program in 1989 to help students pay for housing and food. Two aspects are particularly interesting about Ghana's loan: first, collection of payments is made through the social security system; second, payments do not amount to an extra tax, but postpone payments to the individual's social security account (see Albrecht and Ziderman, 1991). Collecting payments through the social security system is novel, as the other ICL programs discussed here rely either on universities or on the tax collection agency. Ghana's system shows that other entities besides these can collect payments. This is particularly important considering that many under-developed countries collect social security payments but lack an effective tax collection agency. Postponing an individual's payments to an individual's social security accounts is also unique. Rather than charging an extra tax, payments that contributed to the individual's social security account are used to pay for the loan. Paying for education takes precedence over accumulating retirement funds.

Ghana's system has been questioned for its capacity to generate additional resources for the state. Most graduates accumulate maximum retirement benefits before retiring age, but continue making payments until retirement. Therefore, the net effect of the student loan is to redirect some payments from the social security system to higher education, without increasing the amount received by the state. Additionally, the system carries an interest subsidy on the loan, which means that graduates pay back only a fraction of the original amount given to them.

Ghana's ICL is an example of the use of a method different from the tax collection agency for collecting student loan payments in a developing country. The condition that an effective tax collection agency has to exist to collect payments can be relaxed to include other entities that withhold part of an individual's income. This system, however, is also an example that just because payments are being collected the resources of the state are not increasing. Because of its design, a different public entity might end up funding education (in this case, social security). The effectiveness of a cost-recovery mechanism has to be measured according to its capacity to generate additional resources for the state, and by that measure Ghana's original program did not solve the central problem.

Sweden's student assistance program has received considerable attention since its creation in 1965. An importance difference between this program and the others described here is that it intends to finance only student living expenses, as university tuition is covered by the state. The program consisted originally of a combination of a grant and a loan. The repayment mechanism of the loan was modified in 1989 to make it an ICL. The new conditions on the loan asked the student to pay 4 percent of income and carried an interest equal to 50 percent of the government interest rate. Repayments are required until the graduate turns 66, at which moment any outstanding debt is written off (see Reuterberg, 1990). Sweden's loan program is usually considered a successful implementation of ICLs. However, there seems to be relatively little information available that permits a judgment on the success of the program to be made.

Conclusion

The cases studied demonstrate several important topics that have to be considered when implementing HCCs. Yale and Chile show that universities are not ideal collection entities. Yale and New Zealand also warn us against the possibility of students feeling pressed by the market interest rates applied to their education loans – a perception derived from lack of understanding of the time-value of money. Australia and Ghana show that public entities that estimate individuals' incomes can be used successfully to collect payments. All the public initiatives also have in common the lack of interest on the part of private capital to provide funding for their programs.

Common to all these examples is the existence of an entity capable of determining individuals' incomes and collecting payments from them to make the system work. The lack of such an entity makes the implementation of a feasible ICRS very difficult and creates the need for evaluating other alternatives. Such is the case in many developing countries – and, therefore, the capacity of their tax collection agency to determine students' incomes is extremely important when evaluating the possibility of implementing an ICRS in them.

These lessons should aid the implementation of HCCs in developed nations. Some of their features, such as using the tax authorities to collect payments, can be used in the implementation of HCCs in developing countries. These implementation steps are presented in chapter 10.

10 | *Government-driven implementation of human capital contracts*

So far human capital contracts (HCCs) and human capital options (HCOs) have been described as instruments that can develop entirely from private initiatives. For this to happen, as considered in chapter 8, HCCs require developed financial markets and stable legal systems. Whereas those characteristics exist in some (not all) developed countries, a wide range of less developed ones is far from providing a solid institutional platform that can attract investors in HCCs. Furthermore, some developed countries with centralized higher-education systems, like the UK, might be interested in creating arrangements that permitted HCCs to fit within the higher-education sector. A pressing concern for all countries, whether developed or not, is the lack of resources to undertake the many responsibilities they carry. Creating the conditions for private investments in education is an alternative that permits an increase in education investments without tapping into the government's budget. This chapter presents some possible steps that governments could take to facilitate the availability of HCCs for their students.

Institutionalizing human capital contracts

Governments can aid the creation of HCCs by creating a legal infrastructure that takes away the uncertainty concerning the enforceability of the contract and the high costs involved in collecting payments. One such way consists of using the taxing capacity of the state to collect payments from students. Even though payments would be publicly enforced, the investment would still come from private sources. I shall call such an instrument here an "Institutional HCC."

This proposal is based on the experience of other policies that have successfully used the government's tax collection agencies to collect payments other than taxes. Two examples are prominent: first, the implementation of private pension funds (Chile, for example) and, second, several income-contingent loan (ICL) programs that use the tax collection agencies to collect loan payments, such as Australia's Higher-Education Contribution Scheme (HECS) program (see chapter 9). The concept applicable to HCCs is that the state can successfully institutionalize the enforcement of payments to entities other than itself.[1] The resulting collection costs are low[2] and make the investment in education more attractive. The main attributes of this proposal would be: (1) students are charged on an income-contingent basis, (2) private capital invests in the students, with contract parameters set by market forces, and (3) the taxing capacity of the state is used to collect payments.

The ideal Institutional HCC would limit the state's role to enforcing payments, and leave such decisions on how much funding should be provided to each student, what percentage of income to ask, to private investors. In that case, there would be little variation between Institutional HCCs and HCCs, as described in chapters 5, 6, and 7. However, as a first stage, policymakers are likely to have reasons for specifying some of the parameters. For example, to ensure that payments are collected through taxes at a low cost, Institutional HCCs might be implemented only if the same percentage of income was retained from each student. Therefore, the discussion continues assuming that Institutional HCCs are easier to implement if certain parameters are fixed by government.

Consider first a simple plan for implementing Institutional HCCs in which all students have access to a standard contract. The standard contract specifies the percentage of income withheld from the student during a pre-defined period of time. The percentage of income committed, the repayment period, and any other particularities of the contract are common for all students and specified when government creates the regulatory framework for Institutional HCCs. The amount withheld from students is redirected to the private entity or fund that financed part of the student's expenses in the past. Students choose from what fund, if any, to receive financing for their studies. Where they do not receive any money from a fund, no amount is withheld. The following example illustrates this mechanism.

In a given country, Institutionalized HCCs will be implemented and students will have 10 percent of their income withheld for twenty years after graduation. Payments withheld from each student will be directed to the human capital fund that funded that student. Students, upon being admitted to a university, approach human capital funds. After studying each student's situation for future income potential, the human capital fund (HCF) offers a certain amount of money in exchange for the 10 percent that will be withheld upon graduation. Students approach several different funds, looking for the fund that is willing to give them the largest amount of funding for 10 percent of their income for twenty years. Eventually, students chose the fund that offers them the best conditions and receive funding to complete their higher-education studies. Upon joining the workforce, students have a 10 percent standard deduction from their income, which is received by the fund that initially financed them.

The point that stands out about the Institutionalized HCC is that the *only variable is the amount financed*. For example, for a particular student attending a particular university, a fund might be willing to offer US$30,000. However, if the same student decides to attend a university where graduates enjoy higher earnings on average, investors will probably offer a higher amount of funding. Likewise, if the student chooses to attend a school whose graduates earn less, on average, investors will probably offer a lower amount.

The previous example can be expanded beyond the assumption that students receive only one payment from HCFs, and that they are forced to pay regardless of their academic success. Expanding the example is necessary to account for the fact that it is unlikely that students who are just starting their higher education receive only one payment. It is more likely that students will receive periodic payments and therefore the contracts will have to reflect this. Continuing the previous example, contracts could state that the student will receive X amount the first year, Y amount the second year, and Z amount the third year. They would also state what happens where the student does not complete her studies. For example, students who complete only one year of undergraduate work pay 30 percent of the pre-defined percentage of income withheld from students who do graduate, students who complete only two years of undergraduate work pay 55 percent of the pre-defined percentage of income, until after a certain year students pay 100 percent of the pre-defined percentage of income. Although having different percentages of income withheld from different students adds complexity to the system (which Institutional HCCs want to avoid), it is still feasible, considering that in other countries where income-contingent payments are withheld from students the percentage withheld varies from student to student.[3]

From the state's perspective, this Institutional HCC is no more complicated than the withholding of earnings to pay for other services such as health care. It is the simplest alternative because the amount withheld, as a percentage of income, is the same for all those who have gone through higher education and used Institutional HCCs to finance their education. Thus, the implementation is no more complex than that of a graduate tax. Only a distinction between those who have gone through college and received funding and those who have not is needed to make the appropriate deductions.

Steps for implementing Institutional human capital contracts

Once it is accepted that a program such as the one outlined above can be used to implement Institutional HCCs, the following critical steps would be needed to implement it. They should be performed with the goal of attracting private capital to the financing of higher education in mind.

A critical step is determining the parameters that will be used. At this stage, the most relevant questions to answer are: what percentage of income will be withheld from students and how long will the retention last? Estimates like those shown in appendix D (p. 186) should be used to determine what percentage of income will be required from students to provide funding that is sufficient to help them go through university. Other relevant questions include the tax treatment of payments (for example, could other taxes be estimated *after* deducting these payments?) and to which students the funding will be available (all students, only particular groups, etc.?).

Another critical step is designing the complete process of funding and repayment. It includes designing how the student receives the payments (directly or to the university), the information required from the individual while studying, and the method for ensuring that funds collected through the tax collection agency end up in with the HCF that financed the student.

Finally, after determining the parameters of the contract and the operations involved with student financing and repayment, the necessary legal changes that ensure the collection of payments have to be enacted. This stage should include specifying the regulation under which HCFs operate and guarantees offered to them to ensure that they will receive the pre-defined percentage of income from the student during the

Table 10.1 *Design options in the implementation of Institutional human capital contracts*

Step	Design options
Contract parameters	• What percentage of income will be retained from students? • How long will the repayment period be? • Which students will have access to Institutional HCCs? (All, only certain groups) • Is participation mandatory (like a graduate tax), or voluntary? • Will the percentage withheld depend on program completion?
Process design	• How does the student apply for funding? • Who receives the funding (for example, the student or the university)? • Who keeps track of student course completion?
Legal changes	• Who can create Institutional HCFs? • Who will regulate Institutional HCFs? • What guarantees will government give to protect Institutional HCFs?

repayment period. Table 10.1 summarizes some of the alternatives that should be considered by policymakers when designing Institutional HCCs.

The challenges for Institutional human capital contracts

There are at least three barriers for the implementation of Institutional HCCs. First, the willingness of government to enforce payments might not be solid enough from an investor's perspective. Second, there is a risk in using the government to collect other payments than taxes. And, third, the tax collection infrastructure may not be appropriate for collecting the payments due to investors.

The most important concern regarding Institutional HCCs is whether governments inspire enough confidence in investors regarding their willingness to enforce students' payments. For instance, investors will want protection in case the government decides to deduct 8 percent instead of 10 percent of students' income as a result of pressure exerted by power groups (students and young professionals, in this case). In the worst-case scenario, investors may fear that governments simply stop collecting payments from students.[4] An arrangement that protects investors from the political risk involved in their investment would probably be required to ensure the participation of private capital in the program.

Investors will be willing to create HCFs if they perceive that they are not facing risk concerning whether or not the state will actually collect payments. In other words, they will probably be willing to assume income risk from the student (the risk that makes traditional mortgage-type loans less than ideal for financing education) but they will probably not be willing to assume legal or political risk.

The second concern regarding Institutional HCCs lies in the method used to collect the payments. Bruce Johnstone (Johnstone and Aemero, 2000) notes that using tax collection agencies for collecting payments other than taxes is not an advantage inherent in any of the income-contingent proposals, a comment also valid when considering the implementation of HCCs using tax collection agencies. Furthermore, he argues that using tax collection agencies for collecting payments other than taxes carries the inherent political risk of opening an alternative for using the tax collection agency for recovering many different kinds of payments, resulting in additional complexity for the system. In the case of the USA, he also mentions the risk of tampering with the high rate of voluntary tax payment in the country, a comment that can be extended to other countries with high voluntary tax payments.[5]

Whereas it may be true that the USA may face a change in the attitude of its citizens towards paying taxes, this proposal is most valuable in other countries where the tax system is already used for collecting other payments. Chile, for example, collects payments for private health insurance and for private pension funds. Education can be easily justified as one of the other payments that can be included among those made through the tax collection agency. Other countries already deduct amounts from an individual's income earmarked to fund public education institutions.[6]

Johnstone and Aemero (2001) also comment on the difficulty in using any kind of income-contingent mechanism in countries where the tax authorities are unable to collect payments properly, or where individuals have many sources of income. Indeed, if investors cannot track students' income then income-contingent repayment becomes impossible. But even if a country lacks authorities that collect tax payments effectively and accurately determine individuals' income, the program might work for some students. For example, government employees' income can be determined (at least the legal one). Johnstone offers traditional loans and income contingency *only from those students whose income can be tracked* as a possible – though imperfect – solution.[7]

Finally, Institutional HCCs are restricted concerning the percentage of income that a student can commit, and therefore might not be a "complete" solution for the student. For instance, what if the percentage of income committed by the student is not enough to pay tuition and living expenses? If the pre-defined percentage of income that students can commit is not enough to get the student through the university, then the solution provided by Institutional HCCs will only be partial. However, partial help is better than none at all, and the issue is not a good reason for not implementing such contracts. Even if Institutional HCCs cover only partially the costs that students have to bear, they are a step in the right direction towards improving the availability of funds for those who chose to continue studying.

Moving forward

This example of Institutional HCCs is simpler than schemes already in place in other countries, particularly Chile and Australia. Chile's system already incorporates the possibility of discounting different percentages of income from different individuals: different pension funds compete by asking different commissions from individuals. Thus, that system gives the flexibility needed for having personalized discounts, something not even required for Institutional HCCs. Further, Australia's HECS program charges different percentages of income as a function of student's income and collection costs remain low (see chapter 9). Therefore, if the political will exists to enforce payments from students, Institutional HCCs can exist.

Barr (1989, 2001), and Ziderman and Albrecht (1995) have been promoting the idea of collecting income-contingent payments through the state's collection agencies for more than a decade. The fact that tax collection of ICLs is already working successfully in some countries means that HCCs can also be introduced using the same methods.

Further, Institutional HCCs can be even easier to implement than ICLs because they do not require an explicit decision regarding the interest rate charged for student financing.

The critical step that has to be taken to ensure the viability of this proposal is to have governments give as much importance to the collection of this payment as it gives to payments for private pension accounts. Investors and students have to be convinced that all students who receive funds will have a percentage of their income withheld once they join the labor force.

If Institutional HCCs are ever implemented with the successful involvement of the private sector, an important precedent would be set that might help government raise private funds for the financing of primary and secondary education. This possibility is explored below.

State human capital contracts: one step further

So far the discussion around HCCs has centered on higher education. This is the education level where they can be implemented most easily, and also the level of education where investments can be more easily assimilated with individual returns. The theory behind HCCs can be also used for elementary and secondary education, though with some important changes. The remaining part of this chapter will address this possibility.

The problem with basic education

The value of investments in education is higher for primary and secondary education,[8] and thus the best investment opportunities lie in that segment of education. However, HCCs cannot be used directly for investments in primary and secondary education for at least three important reasons. First, there are ethical concerns of having minors commit a portion of their future income. Second, the recovery period for cash flows is much longer, making the investment much more risky. And, third, the externalities derived from elementary and secondary education (see chapter 1) are strong reasons for supporting the government paying for it, keeping the government as the main provider of capital for basic education. This is the reason why Friedman proposed "selling" future income only to finance higher education and vocational training.

There is considerable discussion, however, about the appropriate way in which the state should finance education. The most important distinction is whether government should run schools itself, pay private institutions to run them, or simply pay students to attend the school of their choice. The dominant way in which governments have taken responsibility for basic education is by running the schools themselves. Only recently have the two other options been considered as viable. The private administration of public schools – "charter schools" – has been a recent development in the USA. So has the direct financing of students to attend the school of their choice – school vouchers. These alternatives, however, do not address the problem of where the state obtains the funds for investing in education.

Even if it is accepted that the state should fund elementary and secondary education, governments are usually also constrained to make those investments. Because recent developments such as vouchers and charter schools address only problems of efficiency and choice in the use of resources, under-investment in primary and secondary education is likely to continue unless some innovative alternatives are sought to aid government in its funding. An instrument similar to HCCs could be used to address the problem. The following section describes a possibility for doing so, named here State HCCs.

Description

State HCCs use human capital theory to finance elementary and secondary education. They provide a market-based answer to the value of investing in primary and secondary education and offer an alternative to public debt, releasing government from the risk of additional debt burdens.

Following the argument used for HCCs, it is conceivable that the state could "sell" part of its future personal income tax proceeds to finance an activity that will produce those future tax proceeds. In doing so, the "buyer" of those future tax proceeds would provide the capital needed for making the investment and would bear the risk on it. This can be achieved by offering an investor part of the percentage of income from a student for a given number of years in exchange for capital to finance the student's education. The maximum percentage of income from the student that the state could commit is the effective income tax rate, since above that the state would have to pay more than what is being received from the individual. After engaging in the contract, a fraction of the taxes received from the individual will belong to an investor.

When governments invest today in basic education, they get back part of the value of the investment through the taxes that individuals pay when they join the workforce. From the point of view of the state's finances, the value of the investment in education will be determined by the difference in the present value of tax payments received from the individual with and without basic education.[9]

The value of the investment in education can be negative, neutral, or positive, depending on variables such as income, tax evasion, and tax regulations. If the value is negative, then the government is subsidizing education, and if the value is positive, the government is gaining from the investment. In any case, the state is assuming the risk of the investment in basic education.

The value of the percentage of income that investors would ask in exchange for capital for financing education might be lower, higher, or equal to the value of the difference of the value of tax payments that the state would receive from the individual with and without education. In other words, the value of the investment in education from the point of view of the state, positive or negative, will be reflected in the conditions that investors ask of an HCC. The net present value (NPV) of the investment in education would still fall on the state, but the risk on the value of the investment would be in hands of the investors. Moreover, investors would also make the payments for the investment.

By "selling" part of its future personal income tax proceeds, the state is obtaining resources for investing in education without engaging in debt and without increasing its exposure to the returns of education. The state's payments will be high only when the individual's income is high, and will be low when individuals have small incomes. The results for the state are aligned with the results for the investor.

Implementation

The implementation of State HCCs is relatively simple. Resources are added to accounts by investors willing to provide the capital needed now for someone's education at a given school in exchange for a percentage of their future income. Once students have completed their education, the amount owed to investors is taken directly from the student's taxes. Individuals do not have to pay more taxes, and thus they never see, or even know, how government is financing their attendance at school. The same tax law applies to them as to any other citizen. Students need not know that a previously negotiated amount of their tax payments is going to be paid by the government to the original investor. The negotiation thus takes place only between the state and the investor.

A pure public school model

Every semester (or any relevant period of time for the typical education cycles) private investors make a bid for financing the attendance for one year for students at a particular institution. Public schools[10] interested in participating in the program would publish the tuition cost for the next year, and the number of students they carry in each grade.[11]

With this information investors will make a bid to finance students in a particular school. For example, a bid might look like:

X percent of income for the tuition of each year of Y students in
    Z elementary school

X, Y, and Z are the only variables included in a standardized contract.

If the market develops completely, there should be an offer to finance every spot in every participating school. The percentage of income asked in the bids would vary from school to school, according to the quality and cost of each. At that moment, there are financial resources for anyone who is accepted in the school.

Then, every student (or parents of the student) would seek admission to a school where investors have placed a bid without concern for their financial situation. If the student is accepted, she will be automatically entitled to have her tuition paid by the investor for the following year. As long as the student is in good standing in the school, and bids to finance students in that school are received, the student needs not concern about who is paying for her education.

As an example, assume that there are three schools in the system: A, B, and C. A has 1,000 available spaces, B has 500, and C has 250. Each school has published tuition costs for a year. When the new education cycle comes, government receives the bids shown in table 10.2.

In this case, if bidder 1 wins the bid, he will be entitled to 6 percent of the financed student's income for an agreed period of time, which

Table 10.2 *Example bids for State human capital contracts*

Bid	School	Students	% of income
1	A	600	6
2	A	700	7
3	B	500	9
4	C	250	11

in theory could extend *as long as the student is alive*. The collection would come from the taxes the individual pays during her lifetime.

First, notice that that there were two different bids for school A. In this case, bidder 1 would finance 600 students, whereas bidder 2 would finance only 400, even though the bid was for 700 students. As with any auction, the winner will be the one who charges less. Systems where everybody pays the same, or where everybody gets what they bid, can and should be considered. In this case, let us assume that everyone pays what he bid. Thus, bidder 1 will get 6 percent of the future income of 600 students, and bidder 2 would get 7 percent of the future income of 400 students.[12]

Second, notice the difference in bids according to the school. These differences reflect investors' perceptions of the relation between quality and cost of schools. From their point of view, school C's tuition costs are too high relative to the quality of the school. On the other hand, school A is offering a very competitive price.

Third, the fact that school A is perceived as the best cost/quality school of the three in the example doesn't mean that school A is inexpensive. In fact, it can be the most expensive of all. If this is the case, investors are betting that the future income of students from that school is disproportionate to the cost. The opposite is also true. The fact that investors are asking a higher percentage of income from students who attend school C does not mean that C's costs are the highest in absolute terms. They could well be the lowest. However, bids reflect the perception that even if C is very cheap, the future earned income will be relatively lower than A's. This concept is very important, since this makes funds available for cheap and expensive schools. What would really matter to investors is the relationship between cost and the future income potential of the students who attend that school.

State HCCs make a leap not only to adapt to the conditions of emerging economies, but also to expand the applicability of HCCs to high – school and elementary levels. It does so by switching the players in the contract from student and investor to state and investor. Investors end up having a contract with the state rather than with thousands of individuals, and thus receive only one payment periodically.

The voucher model

State HCCs can also be implemented to fund the school vouchers that government gives to students to choose what school they attend. There are several options to choose from.

Fixed-value voucher

This is the option that most closely resembles current voucher programs. Under this alternative, the government fixes the value of each voucher and students choose the school they attend. If the school is more expensive than the value of the voucher, the student's family pays for the excess cost not covered by the voucher. Investors then would bid on paying the value of the voucher.

Under a fixed voucher value scheme, higher-quality schools (measured by the expected value of the education delivered) will receive bids asking lower percentages of income than lower-quality schools. For example, if the value delivered by school *A* is on average twice as high as the value delivered by school *B*, the percentage of income that investors will demand to finance a student in school *A* will be half as high as the percentage demanded for financing a student in school *B*. This is the result of government's policy to offer the same amount of money for schools that deliver different value.

The fixed value scheme also creates an incentive for the creation of schools of dubious quality with tuition fees similar to the voucher value. Higher tuition costs makes education expensive for students to attend high-quality expensive schools since the family has the burden of paying the difference between the tuition fee and the voucher value. Thus, the fixed voucher value acts only as a discount on the tuition fee; if the remaining fee to be covered by the family is high then the voucher is not making high-quality education more accessible to low-income families.

Table 10.3 *Characteristics of State human capital contracts*

Characteristic	Public school model	Fixed value voucher	Variable value voucher
Schools participating	Public schools	Public and private schools	Public and private schools
Amount investors pay per student	Given	Given	Set by investor auction
Percentage of income determined by	Bid from investors	Bid from investors	Given by the state

Variable-value voucher

As an alternative to vouchers with a fixed value, variable vouchers can be designed to promote access to schools that investors perceive are cheap relative to the value they create to the state, even if they are expensive in absolute terms. To design a variable voucher value scheme, government decides to offer to investors a *fixed percentage of income* from students. Investors would then bid on the absolute amount that they are willing to offer in exchange for that percentage of income.

A variable voucher value scheme makes investors offer different absolute amounts for vouchers to attend different schools. If school *A*'s education value is twice as high as that of school *B*, the voucher to attend school *A* will be half as expensive as that of school *B*. Thus, a variable voucher value scheme *adjusts the effective tuition fee that students pay to the quality of the school they attend*, a desirable consequence that will be discussed later.

Table 10.3 contrasts the three kinds of State HCCs explained above.

Strengths of state human capital contracts

State HCCs provide a source of capital for the education of any person, as long as she is accepted in an educational institution that investors endorse. This keeps the needs and means-blind characteristic of HCCs. It does have the advantage of including elementary and high-school students. Thus, the scope of this alternative is wider than with HCCs. Also, students from different income backgrounds could attend the same expensive schools, as long as the extra cost is compensated by higher value perceived from the point of view of the state.

Education funds like the ones described above would link the life-long value of education with the value of the original investment made in it. HCCs have different return periods, but a very long-term contract, forty years or so, would not be viewed favorably. The kind of contract described in this section does not need to be constrained in time. In principle, contracts like this could be valid until the death of the individual whose education was financed. In doing so, the investor would realize a return on the life-long value of the education received by the individual. Thus, one of finance's golden rules would be fulfilled here: the life of the asset should be matched with the life of the liability.[13]

This type of contract earmarks a fraction of taxes to education, leaving political forces outside the process. The proceeds from taxes are used in a particular kind of investment, an allegedly profitable one. Since private investors have a stake in the use of the investment, they will react to government's changes in education policies and positively influence those who manage the schools to deliver more effective education. Today, pressure on educational institutions to improve their performance depends on other factors influenced only indirectly by private markets.

The percentage of income that investors demand will reflect the cost and the quality of the education received at any particular school. Thus, these contracts would create a market price that discriminates among schools. Moreover, the availability of capital for financing education would spur the creation of private schools. With more students applying for school, and with capital to back them, additional competition could develop at the primary and secondary education level. An increase in competition is positive because prices would be more competitive and students would have more options to choose from.

Furthermore, since the financing of this system comes from the tax payments that the student makes, this kind of contract is not subject to some of the problems found in HCCs. On one hand, since there is no relation between the investor and the student, there is no risk of the undue pressure on the student described in chapter 8. On the other hand, the investor needs to collect only from the state. Since the work that the state does collecting its taxes will probably be taken into account by investors when bidding to finance a student, they will be exposed only to change in the quality of tax collection by the state.

State HCCs have another advantage over HCCs given that the individual would be subject to the same tax treatment as anybody else: no adverse selection. Adverse selection exists only when there is an option for the student where she can retain the upside potential of her investment. Adverse selection does not exist since students will have to pay taxes regardless of the financial scheme they choose. That is, there is no option to pay less. Finally, this alternative does not have the problem of enforceability of contract, since investors are dealing with government, who in turn collects taxes from its citizens.

The hurdles for State human capital contracts

State HCCs face huge political challenges because, unlike Institutional HCCs, they place all the burden of financing education, for those who enter the system, on the state. It is still private funding of education because the state is selling part of the student's future income, but future payments to investors will all come from resources that would otherwise go to the government's Treasury. Thus, there will be a strong political temptation to reject the idea on fiscal grounds – or, worse, to appropriate the payments.

Another hurdle stems from the potentially small value that the state gets back in the form of taxes from the citizens that attend public schools. In Colombia, for example, based on the statistics gathered by DANE,[14] only 4.4 percent of the population receives an income equal or higher to the level where income tax payments are collected. Thus, the state is collecting almost nothing in the form of personal taxes from the resources it devotes to primary and secondary education. In those conditions investors would consider financing only the education of particular public schools – the best ones – asking very high percentages of income from students.

Political and financial challenges might thus prevent the mass creation of State HCCs in the short run. These challenges are not the same in every country, and thus there might be some places where they could actually be implemented. Even if the challenges actually prevent the implementation of this kind of contract, the notion that the state can create contracts where investors take on part of the risk of the value of education could spur the creation of other instruments that could increase the efficiency of government spending. For example, the state could offer contracts to charter schools contingent on the results

Table 10.4 *Contrast between human capital contracts, Institutional human capital contracts, and State human capital contracts*

Characteristic	Human capital contract	Institutional human capital contracts	State human capital contracts
Payment determined as	Percentage of income	Percentage of income	Percentage of income
Payment made by	Student	Student	State
Risk of value of education carried by	Investor	Investor	Investor
Maturity of instrument	10–20 years	10–20 years	For life
Payment to investor	Privately collected	Enforced as compensation discount	Paid from individual's tax payments
Financial help offered to	College and graduate students	College and graduate students	Elementary and high-school students

that their students obtained later in life. These ideas should eventually enable the state to finance better-quality education with the same resources – or, at least, maintain current quality with fewer resources.

Conclusion

Institutional HCCs and State HCCs are an alternative for implementing HCCs in countries where collection costs or unstable legal environments preclude this kind of investment without the support of the state. The proposal builds on the successful experience of several countries in implementing programs for collecting payments using the tax collection agency infrastructure. Because there is value that can be released from enabling capable students to pursue additional education, policymakers can aid in the release of value – social value – by fostering Institutional HCCs.

State HCCs attempt to use human capital theory to increase the amount of funds available for investments in primary and secondary education. This is the stage of education with highest returns and

Table 10.5 *Advantages of different implementations of human capital contracts*

Characteristic	Pure human capital contract	Institutional human capital contracts	State human capital contracts
Creates a source for private funding of education	X	X	X
Shifts risk from student to investor	X	X	X
Instrument is means and needs-blind	X	X	X
Reflects information on the overall return on education	X	X	X
Discriminates between the quality of education	X	X	X
Generates competition among education institutions	X	X	X
Generates competition for funding students	X	X	X
Government intervention required		X	X
Applicable for elementary and high-school education			X
Captures life-long value of education investment			X

thus the stage that can benefit the most from additional investments. State HCCs also expand the possibilities of offering school vouchers to finance education. Fixed value vouchers would not change anything from the point of view of the student, though it would change the perception of value from the point of view of the state. Variable value vouchers would create vouchers whose value depended on the quality of the school the student was attending, increasing access to high-quality and expensive schools to students from low-income backgrounds. Table 10.4 compares HCCs with the implementation proposals brought forward in this chapter and table 10.5 summarizes their main advantages.

11 | *Conclusion*

THE capacity that income-contingent repayment schemes (ICRs) have to transform the traditional way in which governments have faced the challenges of financing education are enormous. The advantages that these repayment schemes offer over other alternatives should lead policymakers around the world to implement the legal structures needed for them to exist.

The process has already started with the introduction of income-contingent loans (ICLs) in several countries. But it cannot stop there. A global market where the value of Human Capital can be traded, in different forms, either directly or through derivative securities, is the ultimate development that can enable capital to flow to wherever there is an opportunity to liberate value by investing in education. That should be the aim of education policymakers around the globe. More than fifty years after Friedman proposed the original idea, the challenge now is whether entrepreneurs and political leaders are willing to use the available technology and the financial innovations that have taken place during that period to serve those who want to invest in education.

The big picture

Towards equal access to education

One of the main arguments in favor of human capital contracts (HCCs) and human capital options (HCOs) is that they can be equally accessible to all, independent of their background. In particular, these instruments should have a special appeal to those that display risk averse behavior towards investments in education and also do not have the resources to invest directly. Students from low-income backgrounds fit this description and are the ones who gain most from this alternative to finance their education. Thus, HCCs and HCOs contribute decisively to create equal access to education.

However, HCCs and HCOs cannot alone solve the problem of un-equal access to education. There are at least two reasons why they alone cannot do the whole work: first, equal access to higher education requires equal access to primary and secondary education; second, some social groups, particularly those from low-income backgrounds, will be systematically misinformed on the value of education, and thus will not be willing to invest in it even if the financial hurdles are cleared.[1] Furthermore, HCCs, by themselves, will not increase the supply for higher education.

Unequal access to primary and secondary education can be the greatest obstacle to offering equal access to tertiary education. As long as particular social groups lack access to an acceptable level of basic education, those same groups will be unlikely to join colleges and universities. To start, they would be rejected from those institutions that required a minimum level or academic achievement. Thus, to solve the problem of access at higher levels of education emphasis has to be placed on basic education. This recommendation complements the observation that the returns to investments in education are highest in elementary education. Primary and secondary education are commonly accepted as the prime responsibility of the state, at least for its financing, and thus this recommendation falls directly on the shoulders of education policymakers. Thus, a government strategy for offering equal access to higher education has to include a government strategy for offering equal access to primary and secondary education. But improving public education to a level where students from different backgrounds are not marginalized from tertiary education will take many years. Thus, the best we can expect is to see equal access improve over time.

Once students complete secondary education, they will be affected by their cultural background on the decision to continue with their education. Certain social groups will be systematically marginalized because of their misinformation on the value of education, and thus will systematically choose to work rather than to invest further in their human capital. A strategy for creating equal access to education has to address this problem by targeting students from these social groups and attracting them. Two possible options for attracting them are (1) the use of scholarships and other financial stimuli, and (2) the creation of specific programs aimed at informing students of the value of education. Scholarships are used not to correct a *financial* deficiency but to correct an *information* problem, and thus complement HCCs, which are aimed to correct a financial deficiency. Information programs may not give out resources to students but are still costly. However, this should be considered as a cost that has to be incurred to achieve the goal of equal access to education.

Thus, HCCs are only one part of a complete strategy to achieve equal access to higher education. This book has been devoted completely to understanding this pillar of a complete strategy without denying the importance of the other pillars. The mechanisms available for improving access to primary and secondary education, and for attracting students systematically misinformed about the value of education, are the subject of other studies, and of further research.

Towards improved higher education

HCCs offer information to the market regarding the value of education, and thus create a new dimension for competition between education institutions. In theory, competition translates into higher quality, lower costs, or both. Thus, the relationship between the value and cost of education improves. However, HCCs alone cannot improve the quality of higher education. The additional information is useless in the absence of mechanisms that permit competition between different institutions to take place.

A complete strategy for increasing the dynamism and quality of the higher-education sector should include mechanisms that increase competition between institutions, for both the best students and for funds. The first step towards increased competition is the existence of a private sector. Other steps are the equal treatment of different institutions regarding financial aid, scholarships, etc., freedom for setting tuition fees, and a competitive labor market. In the absence of these, HCCs and HCOs will still have value as (ICRs) but the information conveyed in their pricing will not yield its most attractive results. Information will still provide an incentive for students in choosing their career and university but will not create additional competition between institutions; it will rather generate disequilibria between the supply and demand for certain institutions and careers. Those that have higher value relative to the cost will see an increase in demand, without a self-adjustment mechanism such as price or the entry of new competing institutions to regulate it.

As with the problem of equal access, HCCs are only one pillar of a complete strategy for improving higher education. The study of the other pillars is not the subject of this book, and thus is not discussed here. However, the reader must keep in mind that the solution presented in this book will be only partial in the absence of the elements that make industries more competitive.

Concluding remarks

The development of human capital theory illuminated the value of human capital, both public and private. Financial theory has provided the tools for valuing human capital – and, perhaps, for trading it. The implementation of ICLs has proved that ICRs schemes can be implemented, by both private and public institutions. The path for implementing HCCs seems to be clear.

HCCs are at the heart of a knowledge society. In such a society the most important asset is human capital, and HCCs can finance its creation by investing directly in it and taking a stake in its value. The benefits of a knowledge society, in theory available to all who have the knowledge, will be limited if knowledge is denied to those who lack capital. HCCs will also enable additional flexibility for investing in continuing education. Investors will be glad to see that the value of their stake in human capital is not depreciating, but rather increasing through continuous retraining. In contrast, lenders, by the nature of their contract with individuals, are not willing to give that flexibility. Thus, the financing of knowledge, from the beginning of a career and throughout an individual's life, is much better suited to be done through HCCs than through other traditional schemes.

But the effects of the introduction of HCCs can extend beyond simply solving a financial problem for students. In absence of debt students might be more inclined to take additional entrepreneurial risks and use their knowledge in ways that they did not dare to before. Friedman's closing words about the original idea of having an "equity" investment in education were:

Existing imperfections in the capital market tend to restrict the more expensive vocational and professional training to individuals whose parents or benefactors can finance the training required. They make such individuals a "non-competing" group sheltered from competition by the unavailability of the necessary capital to many able individuals. The result is to perpet-uate inequalities in wealth and status. The development of arrangements such as those outlined above would make capital more widely available and would thereby do much to make equality of opportunity a reality, to di-minish inequalities of income and wealth, and to promote the full use of our human resources. And it would do so not by impeding competition, destroying incentive, and dealing with symptoms, as would result from the outright redistribution of income, but by strengthening competition, making incentives effective, and eliminating the causes of inequality.[2]

Now that financial and technological developments make the imple-mentation of this concept easier, it is the time for entrepreneurs and policymakers to act. Entrepreneurs can seize the opportunity to create value by enabling individuals to continue their education; policymakers can aid them in creating the legal structure where entrepreneurs and investors can act. Benefits accrue to everyone: those who implement HCCs can derive value from the operation; students have another op-tion, maybe the only one, to finance their education; a country's capac-ity to grow will be enhanced and plausibly those who push for massive financing for higher education will enjoy great popularity among their constituencies.

Appendix A   Valuation of human capital contracts

This appendix develops a framework for valuing human capital contracts (HCCs). This framework should be analytically useful for understanding the behavior of these instruments, as well as for predicting the conditions under which such contracts will be offered in the near future.

The value of a human capital contract

Drivers of value

The main drivers of value in a HCC are: (1) income during the repayment period, (2) percentage of income collected, (3) administration costs, (4) fraction lost due to fraud, and (5) unemployment rate. Without unemployment, the value of a HCC is:[1]

$$HCCV = PVI \cdot \rho - AC - DC \qquad (A.1)$$

where:

$HCCV$ = HCC value
PVI = Present value of student's income during repayment period
ρ = Percentage of income committed by student
AC = Administration costs
DC = Default costs

Unemployment can be included in (A.1) if it is assumed that the probability of being unemployed is evenly distributed during the repayment period. In that case, the present value of the student's income is simply reduced proportionally to the unemployment rate and (A.1) becomes:

$$HCCV = PVI \cdot \rho \cdot (1 - u) - AC - DC \qquad (A.2)$$

where:

u = Unemployment rate

If the administration and default costs are assumed proportional to the value of the contract, then (A.2) can be rewritten as:

$$HCCV = PVI \cdot \rho \cdot (1 - (a + d + u)) \tag{A.3}$$

where:

a = Administration costs as a percentage of the value of the contract
d = Default as a percentage of the value of the contract

It is important to note that the appropriate unemployment rate is not a national average, but rather the one of individuals with similar levels of education. Presumably, their unemployment rate is lower than the national average since higher unemployment rates are observed among lower-skilled individuals.

The underlying asset that gives value to the HCC is PVI, the present value of the income flows that an individual obtains after graduation. This will equal:

$$PVI = \sum_{t=s}^{s+k} \frac{Y_t}{(1+i)^t} \tag{A.4}$$

where:

Y = Annual earnings by the student
s = Number of periods before the first payment is received
k = Repayment period
i = Discount rate

Using continuous compounding, (A.4) becomes:

$$PVI = \int_s^{s+k} Y(t) \cdot e^{-i \cdot t} \cdot dt \tag{A.5}$$

Or, if $Y(0)$ equals the expected income upon graduation,

$$PVI = e^{-is} \cdot \int_0^K Y(t) \cdot e^{-i \cdot t} \cdot dt \tag{A.6}$$

Equation (A.6) can be expanded to include the expected starting income upon graduation and expected income growth during the repayment period. If $Y(t) = Y_s \cdot G(t)$, where Y_s is income upon graduation and $G(t)$ is the income growth function, then (A.6) becomes:

$$PVI = Y_s \cdot e^{-i \cdot s} \cdot f(i, K, G(t)) \tag{A.7}$$

where:

$$f(i, K, G(t)) = \int_0^K G(t) \cdot e^{-i \cdot t} \cdot dt$$

This transformation is also convenient because the expected income upon graduation is a value that can be measured directly.

Equation (A.3), the value of a HCC, becomes:

$$HCCV = \rho \cdot Y_s \cdot e^{-i \cdot s} \cdot f(i, K, G(t)) \cdot (1 - (a + d + u)) \tag{A.8}$$

The price of the contract: required percentage of income

To determine the percentage of income that investors will require from students in exchange of capital, the cost of attending the university has to be combined with the value of the contract. Investors will engage in the contract only if its value is more than the amount they are giving to the student to cover education and living expenses. The profit an investor obtains is:

$$P = HCCV - C \tag{A.9}$$

where:

P = Profit from investment
C = Present value of amount disbursed by investor

In a competitive market, profits are small and investors can only obtain a return on their investment that reflects its risk. If the discount rate used to value HCCs reflects the risk of the investment, then profits should be small or zero. This can be used to estimate the "competitive market" percentage of income that investors would demand in exchange for financing education. At least, it can be used to estimate the minimum percentage of income that investors would demand. If profits are zero, then (A.9) becomes:

$$HCCV = C$$

Or, substituting in (A.8)

$$P \cdot Y_s \cdot e^{-i \cdot s} \cdot f(i, K, G(t)) \cdot (1 - (a + d + u)) = C \qquad (A.10)$$

The percentage of income that investors will demand will be:

$$\rho = \frac{C \cdot e^{i \cdot s}}{Y_s \cdot f(i, K, G(t)) \cdot (1 - a + d + u))} \qquad (A.11)$$

Or:

$$\rho = \frac{C}{Y_s} \cdot e^{i \cdot s} \cdot \left(\frac{1}{f(i, K, G(t))} \right) \cdot \left(\frac{1}{1 - (a + d + u)} \right) \qquad (A.12)$$

Finally, the price of the HCC – the percentage of income *per dollar* financed – can be deduced from (A.12). The price of an HCC is:

$$\frac{\rho}{C} = \frac{e^{i \cdot s}}{Y_s \cdot f(i, K, G(t)) \cdot (1 - (a + d + u))} \qquad (A.13)$$

As would have been expected, income growth and the repayment period will have an impact on what percentage of income students will have to commit. The precise impact, however, depends on the shape of income growth. Finally, administration costs, default rates, and unemployment all add up to make the instrument more expensive for the student. Eventually, any of these factors can make the instrument prohibitively expensive for students if their levels get to be too high.

Equation (A.12) and (A.13) are general solutions for valuing a HCC. It is important to remember the assumptions embedded in these equations:

- Administration and default costs are proportional to the amount owed by the student during the whole repayment period
- Income to the former student and payments to the investor are continuous
- Income growth is only a function of time
- Unemployment is evenly distributed throughout the repayment period
- Competitive markets force risk-adjusted profits to zero.

A Mincerian solution to the general expression

There are several models that relate income to time and education, of which Mincer's human capital earnings function (HCEF) has been increasingly accepted. This well-known model can be used to find a solution to the expressions found in the previous section. Using Mincer's HCEF can be valuable to estimate the pricing of HCCs because studies that estimate its parameters for different countries abound. This section explores a solution using a simplified version of Mincer's HCEF.

According to Mincer (1974), income can be modeled as:[2]

$$\ln Y = \ln B_0 + r \cdot s + h \cdot t - g \cdot t^2 \tag{A.14}$$

where:

Y = Income after t time of experience and s years of schooling
B_0 = Income with no education and no experience
s = Years of schooling
t = Years of experience
r = Rate of growth of income for each additional year of education
h = Rate of growth of income for each additional year of experience
g = Factor that decreases income growth over time; $g \geq 0$

Income during period t, then, can be expressed as:

$$Y(t) = B_0 \cdot e^{r \cdot s} \cdot e^{h \cdot t - g \cdot t^2} \tag{A.15}$$

By defining

$$Y_s = B_0 \cdot e^{r \cdot s} \tag{A.16}$$

Equation (A.15) can be rewritten as:

$$Y(t) = Y_s \cdot e^{h \cdot t - g \cdot t^2} \tag{A.17}$$

Which means that, using Mincer's equation,

$$G(t) = e^{h \cdot t - g \cdot t^2}$$

Substituting $G(t)$ into (A.6), PVI equals:

$$PVI = e^{-i \cdot s} \cdot Y_s \cdot \int_0^K e^{(h-i)t - g \cdot t^2} \cdot dt \tag{A.18}$$

Equation (A.18) can be rewritten to resemble the familiar cumulative distribution function as:

$$PVI = Y_s \cdot e^{-i \cdot s} \cdot e^{\frac{1}{2}\left(\frac{\mu}{\sigma}\right)^2} \sigma \cdot \sqrt{2 \cdot \pi} \cdot \frac{1}{\sqrt{2 \cdot \pi}} \cdot \int_0^K e^{\frac{-(t-\mu)^2}{2 \cdot \sigma^2}} \cdot dt \qquad (A.19)$$

where:

$$\sigma = \sqrt{\frac{1}{2 \cdot g}}$$

$$\mu = \frac{h - i}{2 \cdot g}$$

The result of this equation is:

$$PVI = Y_s \cdot e^{-i \cdot s} \cdot e^{\frac{1}{2}\left(\frac{\mu}{\sigma}\right)^2} \cdot \sigma \cdot \sqrt{2 \cdot \pi} \cdot \left(N\left(\frac{K - \mu}{\sigma}\right) - N\left(\frac{-\mu}{\sigma}\right)\right) \qquad (A.20)$$

where: $N() =$ Cumulative distribution function
Or, substituting for μ and σ,

$$PVI = Y_s \cdot e^{-i \cdot s} \cdot e^{\frac{(h-1)^2}{4g}} \cdot \sqrt{\frac{\pi}{g}} \cdot (N(a) - N(b)) \qquad (A.21)$$

where:

$$a = \sqrt{2 \cdot g} \cdot \left(K - \frac{h - i}{2 \cdot g}\right)$$

$$b = \frac{-(h - i)}{\sqrt{2 \cdot g}}$$

If g is small, then PVI becomes:

$$PVI = Y_s \cdot e^{-i \cdot s} \cdot \int_0^K e^{(h-i)^{-t} \cdot dt}$$

or,

$$PVI = Y_s \cdot e^{-i \cdot s} \cdot \frac{\left(e^{(h-i) \cdot K} - 1\right)}{(h - i)} \qquad (A.22)$$

Table A.1 *Solutions for f(i,K,G(t))*

Assumption $Y = Y_s \cdot e^{h \cdot t - g \cdot t^2}$	$f(i, K, G(t)) =$
$g \neq 0$	$e^{\frac{(h-i)^2}{4 \cdot g}} \cdot \sqrt{\dfrac{\pi}{g}} \cdot (N(a) - N(b))$
	$a = \sqrt{2 \cdot g} \cdot \left(K - \dfrac{h-i}{2 \cdot g} \right)$
	$b = \dfrac{-(h-i)}{\sqrt{2 \cdot g}}$
$g \approx 0$	$\dfrac{\left(e^{(h-i) \cdot K} - 1\right)}{(h-i)}$
$g \approx 0, h \approx i$	K
Second-order Taylor series	$K + \dfrac{(h-i)}{2} \cdot K^2 + \left(\dfrac{(h-i)^2}{6} - \dfrac{g}{3} \right) \cdot K^3$ $\qquad - \dfrac{(h-i) \cdot g}{4} \cdot K^4 + \dfrac{g^2}{10} \cdot K^5$

And if the difference between h and i is small, then PVI is:

$$PVI = Y_s \cdot e^{-i \cdot s} \cdot K \qquad \text{(A.23)}$$

Equation (A.19) can also be solved using Taylor series. The second-order solution would be:

$$PVI = Y_s \cdot e^{-i \cdot s} \cdot \left[K + \frac{(h-i)}{2} \cdot K^2 + \left(\frac{(h-i)^2}{6} - \frac{g}{3} \right) \cdot K^3 \right.$$

$$\left. - \frac{(h-i) \cdot g}{4} \cdot K^4 + \frac{g^2}{10} \cdot K^5 \right] \qquad \text{(A.24)}$$

Equation (A.20), (A.22), (A.23) and (A.24) are all estimates of the value of the present value of income during the repayment period.

Table A.1 summarizes the values that $f(i,K,G(t))$ can have using Mincer's HCEF.

Appendix B   Using human capital options to value income-contingent loans

As shown in chapter 7 human capital options (HCOs) can be used to value income-contingent loans (ICLs). The separation of ICLs into the different instruments that compose them would give policymakers and private investors more flexibility in their design, would permit the allocation of risk to different investors, and would make them easier to trade – and, thus, be more liquid. With this purpose in mind, ICLs are analyzed according to their embedded instruments.

Income-contingent loans type 1: variable payments until the loan is repaid

Market interest rates

This analysis starts with the simplest kind of ICL. This loan has an interest rate r that reflects market rates, asks from the student a percentage of income p each year, and has a maximum repayment period of K years. Each year, the amount owed by the individual is the addition of the accrued interest for the amount owed at the end of the previous period minus the amount the student paid during the current period. If the student still has not repaid the total amount of principal and accrued interest after K years, the remaining balance is forgiven.

This ICL can be separated into two distinct instruments: a loan and an option. This can be understood by studying the amount paid by each student as a function of income. This pay-off structure was shown in chapter 7 and is represented again here in figure B.1.

Students will repay the lesser of (1) the present value of their income during the repayment period times the percentage of income they pay each period, and (2) the present value of the loan and interest. Since it is assumed that this loan has a market-based interest rate, the present value of the loan and interest will equal the amount of the original loan. For those students who pay less than the present value of the

175

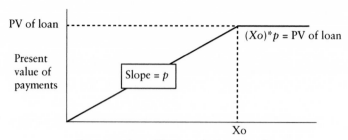

Figure B.1 Income-contingent payments as a function of accumulated income

loan, the present value of their payments will equal the present value of the percentage of income they pay during the repayment period. Students whose present value of income times the percentage they pay is greater than the amount of the loan will pay back the loan. The equation that rules this payment profile is:

$$Payment = \min(p \cdot PVI, L) \tag{B.1}$$

where:

P = Percentage of income paid each period
PVI = Present value of income during K years
L = Loan amount

The same repayment schedule is obtained if the ICL is separated in two parts: a loan and an option

$$Payment_{Loan} = L \tag{B.2}$$

$$Payment_{Option} = -\max(L - p \cdot PVI, 0) \tag{B.3}$$

The negative sign in the second payment shows that the student *receives* the payment from the option. The pay-off for a put option is:

$$Payment_{Put} = \max(S - X, 0) \tag{B.4}$$

where:

S = Strike price
X = Value of the asset when the put expires

Thus, (B.3) is a put option with strike price L and underlying asset $p \cdot PVI$. This option can be interpreted as the student's right to sell a percentage p of his income for K years at the value of the loan L. The underlying asset of this option is a portion of the present value of earnings, or Human Capital, and the expiration time of the option is K. Because students cannot exercise the option of paying only a fraction of their income before the end of the repayment period, this option is a European option.

The value of the ICL is the sum of the value of the loan and the option. From the point of view of the student, the value of the loan is negative and the value of the option positive. Thus,

$$V_{ICL} = -V_L + V_o = -L + V_o \qquad (B.5)$$

where:

$V_{ICL} =$ Value of ICL
$V_L \quad =$ Value of loan
$V_O \quad =$ Value of option

The results from this analysis are not surprising: (1) an ICL will always be less expensive to the student, and thus more valuable, than a loan that has to be repaid entirely, and (2) the valuation of ICLs requires the valuation of Human Capital and its volatility.

Non-market interest rates

The previous analysis revealed the HCOs embedded in two types of ICLs. This section shows that the analysis is still valid when the interest rates are not those offered by the market.

Lower than market interest rates: subsidized loan

The first step is to consider an interest rate lower than that of the market. Because of the policy relevance of higher-education financing, governments might be interested in making conditions on the loan softer than they would be if the market interest rate were offered. This is the case of Australia's and the UK's ICL schemes, where the amount that a student owes is adjusted each year only to reflect inflation. The typical profile of payments against income under this circumstance would be as shown in figure B.2.

The present value of the loan is smaller than the original loan because repayments do not cover the required interest rate. How much the discount on the original amount of the loan is going to be depends

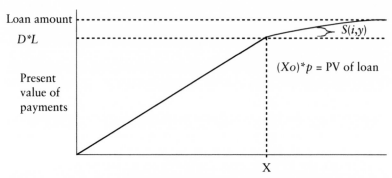

Figure B.2 Income-contingent payments with a subsidized interest rate

on the particular stream of payments made by the individual, which in turn will depend on the individual's income. In general, students with higher incomes during the life of the contract will pay more than students with lower incomes, although there can be exceptions.[1] The maximum amount that a student will pay is limited by the original amount of the loan. If the student is not forgiven any part of the loan the minimum payment is the amount of the loan discounted by a factor that depends on the interest rate of the loan and the would-be interest rate in market conditions. The discount factor can be approximated to:

$$D = e^{k(r-i)}$$

where:

D = Discount factor
K = Maximum repayment period
i = Market interest rate
r = Loan interest rate

Thus, students who repay their obligation in full will pay a present value amount between the amount of the loan L and the discounted amount D^*L. This subsidy can be considerable. For example, a loan with a maximum repayment period of twenty years and a subsidized interest rate 4 percentage points below the market value would offer students a maximum subsidy of 55 percent of the original value of the loan.

The subsidized ICL can be divided into three different instruments: (1) a discounted loan with a market interest rate, (2) an option, and (3) an extra payment that depends on the particular income stream of the student. The discounted loan and the extra payment are not easy, though not impossible, to separate. But the option can still be separated from the rest of the loan. The value of the loan will be:

$$V = -D \cdot L + V_o - S(i, y_t) \tag{B.6}$$

where:

V = Total value of the loan
V_o = Value of the option
S = Value of the "extra charge"
i = Difference between loan interest and market interest
y = Earnings profile

The conclusion is that an ICL with subsidized interest rates can still be divided into a loan and an option. The option is an HCO because its value depends on an individual's stream of earnings; the subsidized loan will depend on the subsidized interest rate and on human capital. Admittedly, the value of the subsidized loan is still difficult to value, but what is of interest for the purpose of this book is that the risk of the option can be separated from that of the loan.

Higher than market interest rates[2]

ICLs can also be offered with higher than market interest rates. This kind of loan attempts to compensate the loss that the loan will produce for those who have a fraction of their loan forgiven, with a gain for those who end up with higher life-long earnings. This option produces undesirable results, as can be seen in figure B.3.[3]

The results are undesirable because the value of payments increases with the time required by the individual to repay the debt, causing high-income individuals, who repay fast, to pay less than other lower-income individuals. Thus, this policy makes middle-income earners pay more than low-income and high-income ones.

Regardless of the inequitable results that charging higher than market interest rates would produce, the division of this instrument into a loan and an option is almost identical to the previous example. The option is identical, while there are only two differences in the loan. First, the present value of the loan will be higher than the actual loan

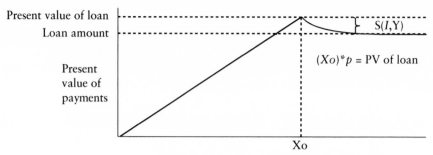

Figure B.3 Income-contingent payments with higher than market interest rates

amount. And, second, high-income earners receive a subsidy rather than being charged an extra amount over the present value of the loan. However, because higher than market interest rates are asked from students precisely to recover the value of the option, different alternatives where the value of the option is explicitly recognized should displace this particular kind of loan.

Income-contingent loans type 2: fixed periodic payments with low-income protection

Another type of ICL is a loan where the student has to pay *each period* the lesser between (1) a percentage of income, and (2) a fixed amount. This type of ICL is the one used in Chile, where students have to pay the maximum between a fixed amount and 5 percent of their income each month. Further, a human capital contract (HCC) in which payments are capped would be equivalent to this arrangement. The payments that the student makes *each period* are shown in figure B.4.

The equation that describes the payments that the student has to make each year is:

$$Payment_t = \min(p \cdot I_t, F) \tag{B.7}$$

where:

P = Percentage of income
I_t = Income in period t
F = Maximum payment for each period

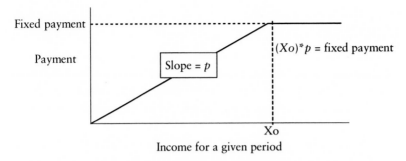

Figure B.4 Income-contingent payments each period, market interest rate

This payment profile is analogous to the previous example. The difference is that there is one option *for each* scheduled payment. Thus, the value of this ICL can be calculated by dividing the instrument in two parts: a loan and a series of options.

The value of the loan is the present value of a constant cash flow of F. The fixed payment can be set to equal the periodic payments that the student would have to make to repay a loan of value L at a competitive interest rate. In that case, the present value of receiving F during the life of the loan is L.

The value of the options is the sum of each option:

$$V_O = \sum_{i=1}^{n} V_i \tag{B.8}$$

where:

V_i = Value of the option of period i
n = Number of scheduled payments during the life of the loan

And the value of the loan will be:

$$V_L = -L + V_O \tag{B.9}$$

The conclusion derived from the ICL with a maximum repayment period applies to this ICL. Basically, this ICL is more valuable for the student than a loan with a fixed payment, reflecting the fact that the student has an option, which has value.

Non-market interest rates

ICLs that have maximum yearly payments are easier to interpret than the ICLs with a maximum total repayment amount. This is because the interest rate is reflected in the maximum periodic payments, giving the same present value of the *loan* for every debtor, regardless of their income. As with loans that reflect market interest rates, each year the student pays the lesser of (1) the fixed amount, and (2) the percentage of income committed. The pay-offs of this kind of option will be like those of figure B.4, regardless of the interest rate.

A simple model for valuing human capital options

The value of options depends on many parameters, particularly on the behavior of the value of the underlying asset. A simplified solution for the value of the option can be estimated using the Black–Scholes (1973) option-pricing model.[4] The results obtained in this section are useful for analytical purposes, and as a starting point in the valuation process. However, because the assumptions underlying the Black–Scholes model are far from being completely satisfied, these expressions should be considered approximations. The assumptions underlying the Black–Scholes model include (1) Brownian motion in the value of the underlying asset – in other words, returns should be log normally distributed, (2) "frictionless markets," i.e. markets with no transaction costs, where short sales are allowed and borrowing and lending can be done at the same rate, and (3) a constant interest rate during the life of the contract. None of these assumptions is satisfied completely in this case.

The Black–Scholes option-pricing model is summarized by the formula that prices an option:

$$V_c = S \cdot N(d_1) - e^{r_f \cdot t} \cdot X \cdot N(d_2) \tag{B.10}$$

$$d_1 = \frac{\ln\left(\frac{S}{X}\right) + \left(r_f + \frac{\sigma^2}{2}\right) \cdot t}{\sigma \cdot t^{1/2}} \quad \text{and} \quad d_2 = d_1 - \sigma \cdot t^{1/2}$$

where:

V_c = Value of call option
S = Underlying asset value
X = Strike price
r_f = Risk-free rate

σ = Volatility of the underlying asset
t = Time to maturity of the option
$N(\ )$ = Cumulative normal distribution function

Once the value of the call option has been determined, the value of a put option can be computed using the following formula:

$$V_p = V_c - S + X \cdot e^{-r_f \cdot t} \tag{B.11}$$

where:

V_p = Value of a put option

The parameters for valuing HCOs[5] in income-contingent loans where the student has to pay a percentage of income until the amount is completely repaid (type 1 in this appendix) are:

Underlying asset value = $P \cdot PVI$
Strike price = L
Expiration time = K
Volatility = $\sigma(PVI)$
Risk free = Risk-free interest rate for K years

For HCOs in ICLs where the student has to pay each period the minimum of a percentage of income and a fixed amount (type 2 in this appendix), the parameters are:

Underlying asset value = $p \cdot I_i$
Strike price = F
Maturity = i
Volatility = $\sigma(I_i)$
Risk free = Risk-free rate with maturity i

The factors that affect the value of the option are the value of income, the strike price, the time to maturity, the interest rate, and the volatility of income. Thus, not surprisingly, the valuation of ICLs requires the valuation of Human Capital and its volatility. This will probably be true after more complex valuation techniques are used. The most important difference between both types of ICLs discussed above is that the "variable repayment period" ICL (type 1) requires estimating the value and volatility of Human Capital only once, while the "fixed payment" ICL (type 2) requires periodic estimates of income and volatility during the repayment period.

Appendix C   Features of human capital contracts, income-contingent loans, and traditional mortgage-type loans

Table C.1 *Features of human capital contracts and income-contingent loans*

Feature	Human capital contract	Income-contingent loans type 1[a]	Income-contingent loans type 2[b]	Mortgage-type loans
Payment	Percentage of income	Percentage of income until loan is repaid or maximum repayment period reached	Lesser of (1) a percentage of income, and (2) a fixed payment	Fixed
Maturity	Fixed	Variable (up to a maximum)	Fixed	Fixed
Repayment amount	Variable	Lesser of (1) present value of a percentage of income, and (2) loan amount	Present value of loan minus the amount by which any periodic payment fell below the fixed payment value	Loan amount
Subsidy	No subsidy necessary	• External (government, non-profit, etc.) • Mutualized (premium from high earners covers losses from low earners)	• External • Mutualized (high interest rate to cover for lower payments)	External
Risk of returns on investment[c]	Student and investor	• Student • Subsidizing agency • Other students in pool	• Student • Subsidizing agency • Other students in pool	Only student

Notes:

[a] The student pays a percentage of income until the loan and interest is fully repaid or until the maximum repayment period is reached.

[b] The student pays each period the lesser of (1) a fixed payment, and (2) a percentage of income.

[c] Assuming no default risk.

184

Table C.2 *Human capital contracts and income-contingent loans versus traditional mortgage-type loans*

Advantage	Human capital contract	Income-contingent loans type 1	Income-contingent loans type 2	Mortgage-type loans
Uses future earnings as source of education financing	X	X	X	X
Can be used to create a source for private funding of education	X	X	X	X
Protects students against low income	X	X	X	
Instrument is means and needs-blind	X	X	X	
Shifts risk from student to investor	X	X	X	
Reflects information on the expected value of education	X	X*	X*	
Discriminates according to the quality of education	X	X*	X*	
Generates competition among education institutions	X	X*	X*	
Adds liquidity to investments in education	X	X*	X*	

Note:
* In less degree than pure HCCs.

Appendix D A developing country study

This appendix uses the results obtained in appendix A to estimate the values that human capital contracts (HCCs) would have in Colombia. The value of finding a solution using Mincer's human capital earnings function (HCEF) can be seen here, since studies that estimate Mincer's parameters are widely available. A similar analysis can be run where measurements of the parameters of the HCEF are available.

Parameters of valuation

The following parameters were used to estimate the values that HCCs could take in Colombia. The value of expected income depends on statistical information on income, education, and experience; unemployment and default are estimated using macroeconomic data; costs can be found by gathering university tuition cost information; and the appropriate discount rate can be estimated from information on the risk premium that the country's debt faces.

Value of expected income

Núñez and Sánchez (2000) use the most widely available source of income information to estimate the returns of education in Colombia. They characterize the parameters of the Mincerian equation presented in appendix A:

$$\ln Y = \ln Y_0 + r \cdot s + h \cdot t - g \cdot t^2 \tag{D.1}$$

A small adjustment needs to be made to their parameters, however, because they used age rather than the time after graduation to determine income.[1] Thus, the equation they solve is:

$$\ln Y = \ln Y_0 + r \cdot s + h \cdot l - g \cdot l^2 \tag{D.2}$$

where:
$l = $ age

Table D.1 *The human capital earnings function in Colombia*

Variable	Value
ln Y_0	9.837
r	0.102
h	0.0757
g	0.0008
Gender dummy variable[a]	0.4211

Note:

[a] The regression used in this exercise is the one that according to Núñez (2000) results in the highest R^2. The gender coefficient implies that males have higher starting salaries for the same level of education and experience.

Following the same steps as in appendix A, defining A as the age at graduation, and manipulating (D.2), income t years after graduation can be expressed as:

$$Y(t) = Y_0 \cdot e^{r \cdot s + A \cdot h - g \cdot A^2} \cdot e^{(h - 2 \cdot A \cdot g) \cdot t - g \cdot t^2} \tag{D.3}$$

The expected income at graduation would then be $(t = 0)$:

$$Y_{s,A} = Y_0 \cdot e^{r \cdot s + A \cdot h - g \cdot A^2} \tag{D.4}$$

And (D.3) can be expressed as:

$$Y(t) = Y_{s,A} \cdot e^{(h - 2 \cdot A \cdot g) \cdot t - g \cdot t^2} \tag{D.5}$$

Equation (D.5) has the same form as (A.17) in appendix A, and thus the value of expected income, or PVI will be[2]:

$$PVI = Y_{s,A} \cdot e^{-i \cdot s} \cdot e^{\frac{(h - 2 \cdot A \cdot g - i)^2}{4 \cdot g}} \cdot \sqrt{\frac{\pi}{g}} \cdot (N(a) - N(b)) \tag{D.6}$$

And,

$$a = \sqrt{2 \cdot g} \cdot \left(K - \frac{h - 2 \cdot A \cdot g - i}{2 \cdot g} \right)$$

$$b = \frac{-(h - 2 \cdot A \cdot g - i)}{\sqrt{2 \cdot g}}$$

Nuñez and Sánchez (2000) present the following results shown in table D.1 in their paper.

Table D.2 *Initial earnings statistics*

Parameter	Men	Women
A	23	23
$Y_{s,A}$ (monthly, Colombian pesos)	544,705	357,503
$Y_{s,A}$ (annual, US$dollars)	5,344	3,507

The parameters' units produce as a result monthly income in 1998 Colombian pesos. Using the average daily exchange rate for 1998, 1,427.04 Colombian pesos per dollar,[3] and an assumed graduation age of 23 years, the parameters to be used in (D.6) are shown in table D.2.

Contract parameters

The design of the contract will affect the percentage of income that students will have to pay in two ways: first, the repayment period of the contract and, second, the number of years that are being financed.

In determining the repayment period of the contract, several forces that act in opposite directions have to be balanced. On the one hand, the optimal financing period for an HCC should match the life of the investment, which in this case equals the productive life of the individual. On the other hand, however, investors, and presumably students, wish to conclude the contract as soon as possible. Thus, an intermediate repayment period should be used. With these factors in mind, the entrepreneurs who have launched HCCs in the USA have used ten and fifteen years as repayment periods.

Another important factor for determining the repayment period is the relationship between income growth and the discount rate. If income growth is higher than the discount rate used by investors, then there is a benefit in prolonging the contract if the other variables remain constant, since the present value of each year's repayments will be higher than that of the previous one. As a result, the proportion of income that a student has to commit decreases *less than linearly proportionally* as the repayment period grows. Or, as a numeric example, if students need to commit 10 percent of their income with a repayment period of ten years, they will need to commit less than 5 percent for a twenty-year repayment period. If, on the other hand, income growth is lower than the discount rate, prolonging the contract does not add much value, since each additional year's income will be less valuable than the previous one. In this case, the proportion that a student has to commit decreases *less than proportionally* as the repayment period grows. Following the lines of the previous example, if students need to commit 10 percent of their income with a repayment period of ten years, they will need to commit more than 5 percent for a twenty-year repayment period. Thus, in circumstances where growth is small relative to the discount rate, shorter repayment periods will yield better conditions for investors and students.

Because HCCs will presumably be discounted at higher discount rates in Colombia than in the USA, shorter periods of time are considered for this exercise. This example considers repayment periods of three to ten years. This decision reflects the consequences of having higher discount rates and the time frame that local capital markets are used to managing.

The second relevant variable in the design of the contract is the period before the investor receives the first payment. This period will range between one and five years, depending on the moment of a student's career that an investor starts providing capital. The most attractive market, from the investor's point of view, is that of students who are in their last university year but lack the resources to conclude their studies. These students will start earning in a relatively short period of time and have an academic track record that decreases risk for investors. The least attractive market, on the other hand, is that of freshmen beginning long careers. These students have only their academic record during school to offer as information about themselves and will start repaying in a relatively long period of time.

All levels of education have the potential to be financed through HCCs. However, freshmen will get less attractive conditions than seniors. To show that HCCs can be used to finance the *whole* career, this example will assume five years of education. If the results obtained with this assumption seem plausible, then students who are more advanced in their studies will get even better conditions.

Unemployment and default

The calculation of the present value of income does not take into account unemployment and default. To estimate unemployment, the

Table D.3 *Participation in the informal sector, by education level*

Education level	Participation in the informal sector (1998) (%)
Incomplete primary	72
Complete primary	57
Incomplete secondary	52
Complete secondary	32
Incomplete college	18
College and higher	10

average of the last ten years is used for the age group with lowest unemployment: 25–55 years. Although in the model students are expected to graduate at 23 and 21 years for professional and technical universities, respectively, their unemployment level throughout most of the repayment period falls in the 25–55 age range. Also, this information does not discriminate between education levels. Assuming that college graduates have lower unemployment rates than non-graduates, their unemployment level should be lower than that of the whole group. Thus, it is conservative to assume that they will fall under the average unemployment rate. According to Colombia's Statistics Center, DANE, unemployment for the period between 1991 and 2000 was 9.1 percent.[4]

The estimation of default is more elaborate. To estimate default, Núñez (2001) is used to determine the feasibility of collecting payments from professionals in a country with high fiscal evasion like Colombia. On p. 15 of his report, Núñez presents a table that estimates the participation of different groups in the informal sector of the economy. His results are presented in table D.3.[5]

Thus, although an estimated 60 percent of the Colombian population is employed in the informal sector, only 10 percent of college graduates actually join. The remaining 90 percent declare income or are affiliated to the Social Security System, and thus have an income that can be determined to collect payments. Since the Mincerian model used for this example is based on what people report that they earn, differences between what they really earn and what they report they earn are already taken into account.

The real default rate will not equal 10 percent because some individuals who join the informal sector might pay back their obligations and others who join the formal sector might refuse to do so. Because it is likely that individuals who join the informal sector do not pay their obligation, default is likely to be higher than 10 percent. For this example, a 5 percent default above the 10 percent estimated in the previous paragraph will be used. Thus, the expected default rate used here is 15 percent.

Discount rate

The appropriate discount rate that investors would use to evaluate investments in human capital in Colombia will vary, depending on the development of these contracts. The first attempts are experiments made with no previous experience. This demands high discount rates. The use of high discount rates would make the cost of HCCs prohibitive except for a few cases of very high-income potential students without the resources to complete their careers. However, as investors learn from their experiments, and as the volume of students financed through HCCs increases, the discount rate should decrease to reflect the decrease of "inexperience" risk. Eventually, the discount rate should stabilize at a level that reflects the risks from investing in education. As discussed in chapter 1, a discount rate of 8 percent can be used for investments in education. Because this example shows how HCCs would be priced when they were a viable alternative for massively financing higher education, the 8 percent discount rate will be used.

To the rate that reflects the risk of investments in education, a premium has to be added to reflect country risk. This premium can be estimated from the premium that government bonds pay above the US cost of borrowing. Colombia's debt rating on November 9, 2001 was BB[6] with a risk premium over 10 year foreign national debt if 504bps.[7] Thus, the following example will use a nominal 13 percent discount rate.

A final adjustment is made to the nominal discount rate to obtain the real discount rate. Real rates should be used in this example because the Mincerian equation solved in this chapter relates real income and income growth to years of education and age. Using a long-term inflation rate of 3 percent, the real discount rate used for this example will be 10 percent.

Table D.4 *Required percentage of income per US$1,000 financed*

	Professional five-year degree (%)	Technical three-year degree (%)
Men	5.7	6.1
Women	8.7	9.3
Arithmetic average	7.2	7.7

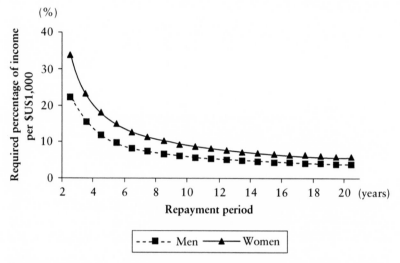

Figure D.1 Variation of required percentage of income with repayment period

Results

The feasibility of implementing HCCs can be assessed by evaluating the required percentage of income that students would have to commit in order to finance their education. Table D.4 shows some of the findings.

The graph in figure D.1 shows the variation in the percentage of income required with respect to the length of the contract. It can be seen in the graph that a ten-year repayment period can be convenient because the change in the required percentage of income gained from increasing by one year the repayment period are relatively small.

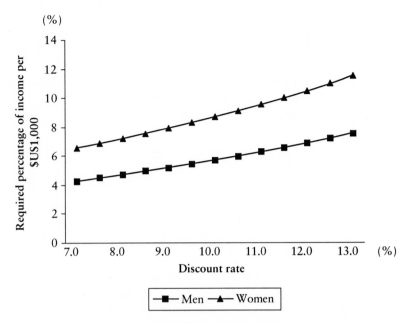

Figure D.2 Required percentage of income as a function of the discount rate

The impact of variations in the discount rate is very relevant. A percentage point change can improve conditions for HCCs in very favorable ways. Figure D.2 shows how the required percentage of income varies according to the discount rate.

In general, a change in the country risk of 200bps such as the one Colombia suffered during 2001 changes the percentage of income that investors would ask to engage in a HCC by 1 percent and 1.5 percent for men and women, respectively. The cost of increasing country risk is very high for this project.

The impact of a variation of 10 percent in any of the variables, while maintaining the others constant, is depicted in figure D.3. This graph is useful for understanding which variable has the highest impact on the percentage of income that investors would ask students to commit.

The income that a student obtains upon graduation has the highest impact on percentage of income. This should be no surprise, since this value is very important given the relatively low growth rates of income with time. Thus, when planning the implementation of HCCs, it is the variable that has to be most carefully measured and estimated.

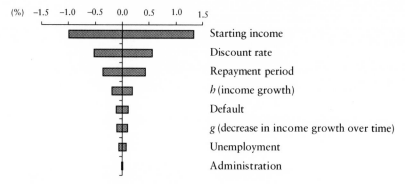

Figure D.3 Relevant drivers of value

Discussion of results

Under the parameters used for this example, students would have to commit on average 7.2 percent, and 7.7 percent respectively, of their income for ten years to finance $1,000 for five and three years of education, respectively. This information has to be contrasted with actual education costs to estimate what impact this would have on the student.

López (2001) presents estimated costs for five- and three-year programs. His estimates are 1,700,000 Colombian pesos of 2000 as the semester tuition fees for five-year professional careers and 1,000,0000 Colombian pesos of 2000 for three-year technical careers. Though probably the solution to the Mincerian equation would have different values for professional careers and technical careers, this analysis will assume that the same equation can be used to analyze both.

Using the average exchange rate between the Colombian peso and the US dollar, the total percentage of income that a student would have to commit to pay for first-year tuition as a freshman is 11.7 percent to start a professional career and 7.4 percent to start a technical career. At this level, the cost of paying tuition for the whole career would be prohibitive, because the commitment of high percentages of income on the part of the student is not desirable. López (2001) suggests 16 percent of income as an appropriate level and MyRichUncle™ is not willing to finance above 15 percent of income.[8] Thus, as presented in this example, HCCs will only *partially* cover education costs, at least at the beginning.

Assuming that students graduate after committing 16 percent of their income, HCCs could finance 35 percent of the tuition of professional careers and 84 percent of the tuition of technical careers.[9] Going further, assuming that the other direct costs that students have to pay equal Colombia's minimum salary, then tuition would represent around 60 percent of total costs.[10] Thus, HCCs could finance around 21 percent of higher education costs for professional careers and 50 percent of costs for technical careers. This contribution, though not substantial, is not marginal either. As the system develops and (1) better information is available by university and career, (2) a higher percentage of income can be asked from the individual, and (3) longer repayment periods are used, the contribution can be expected to increase to higher levels.

These findings may surprise the reader, but they are the consequence of using the same equation to estimate earnings while using very different yearly tuition costs. These results would reflect reality if the difference in tuition did not reflect a difference in the value of education offered by technical and professional universities. Further research can study whether such difference in tuition costs are justified.

Conclusion

The values obtained above show that a scheme that uses HCCs and HCOs can be implemented, even if not covering 100 percent of the costs in Colombia. The same methodology can be used to seek feasibility in other countries.

When choosing between professional and technical universities, with the information now available HCCs would be much more valuable for technical higher education institutions than for professional ones. This result calls for further research, because for it to hold students from both professional and technical universities must be grouped in one Mincerian equation. Statistical research that shows the relationship between earnings upon graduation and the type of career could offer more precise information.

Some caveats need to be added. First, the use of macroeconomic data permits us to make only a country generalization and, second, the model can still be refined to a much more precise level to include other relevant variables.

The first caveat is needed because as this example used macroeconomic data, these results are valid only at an aggregate level. In reality, graduates from different universities and different careers have different HCEFs and would be offered different conditions by investors willing to invest in human capital. But if at the aggregate level there are indications that an implementation could work, at a less aggregated level there must be very attractive opportunities. Thus, these results should prompt additional interest for investing in human capital in Colombia.

The second caveat reflects the fact that the dynamics of student financing requires the inclusion of, among other variables, desertion rates and average completion time. Investors can reduce their risk by starting with students who are already in their third or fourth year of study – students whose completion date is more certain and whose desertion rate is lower. These were not included here to not distract the reader from the main drivers of the model. For more detail, the valuation appendix (appendix A, p. 167) does include these parameters.

The next step for implementing such a system is to perform research at a university and career level that, at least partially, permits us to determine how starting salaries and costs compare between universities and careers, and how the volatility of those earnings behaves. With this information the feasibility of particular programs at several attractive universities can be evaluated and then the most promising can be implemented as pilot programs.

Notes

1 The value of education

1. The consequence of this is that there is no quantifiable *optimal* level of investment in education. The optimal amount will depend on the value placed by society on the qualitative benefits of education.
2. See Griliches (1977) for some of the problems of measuring returns to schooling, particularly regarding the omission of ability. The effect of inheritance in earnings is also studied in Mulligan (1999). For a different perspective, see Blackburn and Neumark (1995).
3. Becker (1993, 210).
4. See Azariadis and Drazen (1990).
5. Thurow (1996, 68).
6. Thurow (1996, 72).
7. The relative value of the costs of investing in education can be surprising and are often ignored. For instance, tuition usually represents a relatively small percentage of the whole investment while forgone earnings are a relatively large portion of the total cost. Table 1.1 shows the share of tuition in schooling expenses for students in several countries. When all the costs are included in an analysis of investing in education, some often overlooked consequences are highlighted. A very interesting one is that professions requiring more years of education dramatically increase total costs, making the investment less attractive. From a financial point of view, therefore, the length of education required of such professions will be a deterrent to students from low-income families. This is a relevant point given the artificial way in which most courses are made longer than necessary. Consider, for example, the typical school calendar in universities with unnecessarily long summers, which time could be used to teach almost an entire additional semester. If tuition represents only 15 percent of the total costs, and assuming a 10 percent discount rate, an institution that reduces a five-year course by one year could raise tuition fees by 130 percent and still leave the total cost for the student constant. Thus, one observed consequence of introducing market-based mechanisms among institutions of higher education is the shortening of the length of programs.

8. Such analysis has to include the tax impact of the investments in education.

9. The name comes from Jacob Mincer, one of the great contributors to human capital theory. Mincer and Becker developed the equation that relates the natural logarithm of income to the number of years of education multiplied by a factor. Under certain assumptions, this factor will equal the average rate of return on education. However, those assumptions are true only in special cases. Mincer then expanded the model to include on the job training in the equation, and the result is what is now known as the human capital earnings function (HCEF) (see Mincer, 1974). For a very informative article on the caution required when evaluating Mincerian returns to education see Chiswick (1997). This paper can be found in http://www.worldbank.org/html/dec/Publications/Workpapers/WPS1700series/wps1790/wps1790-abstract.html.

10. See Psacharopoulos (1994).

11. The information on each individual country is found as an appendix in Psacharopoulos (1994).

12. This rate should be taken as a general guide, still subject to further research. Tehlado and Silva (2001), for instance, show that the risk of investments in education in different countries is correlated with the returns of education, implying that higher returns compensate for higher risk and, therefore, that the appropriate discount rate is different for each country. Their research, however, still does not offer a quantification of the appropriate risk-adjusted benchmark rate to use.

13. This point is taken up again in chapter 6, since an active market for HCCs would enable selling and buying the value of human capital, increasing its liquidity and consequently reducing its discount rate.

14. Marshall (1956, bk. VI, 467–468).

15. The role that HCCs will play in different countries will also be different depending on the returns to investments in education in a particular country. In countries where returns are lowest, which are also the ones where capital markets are most developed, HCCs will offer more choices and information to students. In poorer countries, HCCs will be an alternative for significantly increasing the necessary investments in education without marginalizing the poorest in the process.

2 Market failure in the financing of education

1. Except for the second part of chapter 10, which speculates on a proposal for compulsory education using the instruments argued for in the book.

2. Friedman (1962) calls this "education for citizenship," see chapter 4 below, probably inspired by Aristotle's writings (See Aristotle, 1992).

3. This assumption is important because several of the benefits derived from using HCCs are based on the additional information they produce in the higher-education market, and how that information can be used to achieve greater efficiency in this market.

4. The discussion here about the risks to individuals and investors of investing in education closely follows his argument.

5. Barr (2001) identifies *information poverty* as the problem, rather than *financial poverty*. It is worthwhile to make the distinction, even if these two types of poverty are highly correlated.

6. Several studies have attempted to model the returns of education for those who drop out of college.

7. Consider a game in which you pay $1 for a chance to win $7 if you obtain a six upon throwing a dice. The expected value of this game is:

$$EV = -1 + (1/6)^*7$$
$$EV = 1/6$$

The result being positive, an individual with no risk preference would play this game. Having no risk preference is also expressed as being risk neutral. On the other hand, a risk averse individual might decide not to join. There is a third category comprised of risk-seeking individuals, i.e. those who go for decisions with negative expected values. People who gamble at casinos fall into this category.

8. Possible investors in education include lenders interested in earning a fixed interest and equity investors willing to take risks on the rate of return in exchange for upside potential. The market for equity investors does not as yet exist for education. Thus, the discussion will consider the analysis of investing in education from the viewpoint of a lender.

9. The study of adverse selection started with G. Akerlof's famous paper: "The Market for Lemons: Quality Uncertainty and the Market Mechanism" (Akerlof, 1970).

10. Adverse selection is also a problem for HCCs. This point will be analyzed in detail in chapters 6 and 8.

11. Ironically, mobility also gives more opportunities for individuals to increase their return on the investment in education. Thus, lenders should *promote* mobility and seek alternatives to collect efficiently.

12. This suspicion is present even in a market-friendly country like the USA. An example is the concern that some parents and teachers have

expressed with charter schools, such as The Edison Schools, the largest private operator of public schools in the USA.

13. A striking example is Chile's failed attempt at the beginning of 2001 to sell bonds to the private sector for funding higher education. Students at public universities reacted aggressively to the idea, and called it the "privatization of higher education."

14. Although the discussion around school vouchers shows that the US public is not satisfied with the results of such a system.

3 The need for alternatives to traditional funding

1. See Ziderman and Albrecht (1995).
2. See chapter 8.
3. The different types of vouchers are beyond the scope of this chapter. It should be enough to state that although vouchers increase student choice, government still has some control over how the money is spent. That control comes, among other ways, by dictating what institutions can receive the vouchers and how much above the value of the voucher students can spend.
4. In particular, Australia's Higher-Education Contribution Scheme (HECS) program has apparently not damaged access. (See chapter 10 for more details.)

4 The evolution of human capital contracts

1. "Neighborhood effects" are the benefits that society receives from an educated individual from which the individual cannot benefit. Friedman does recognize some neighborhood effects of vocational and professional schooling, what we would call "social benefits" as defined in chapter 1. However, he states that these benefits are small compared to the private benefits that the individual receives. (See chapter 1.)
2. Friedman (1962).
3. He *does* think, though, that they are the economic equivalent of "partial slavery."
4. This question seems to be in the mind of many economists today, as Gary Becker wrote in a letter to one of the venture capitalists who is trying to make HCCs a reality in the USA (private correspondence from Gary Becker to Roy Chapman, February 28, 1996, cited with the permission of Roy Chapman).
5. This is similar to Yale's program. (See chapter 1.)
6. There are three main types of "buyout" alternatives: (1) target interest rate, (2) multiple of debt, and (3) multiple of debt and interest.

Under the target interest rate design, students pay a percentage of their income until the pool repays its obligations or until the student completes the payments for a loan with a *higher* interest rate than that of the loan given to the pool of students. In other words, the lender offers a pool of students capital at a given interest rate but each student has to repay until (1) the whole group repays the debt or (2) the student has paid her individual loan at a higher interest rate.

The multiple of debt "buyout" design consists of asking students for a percentage of their income until they have paid a multiple of the original amount given to them or until the pool has repaid back the loan at the stipulated interest rate.

Multiple of debt and interest "buyouts" work in the same way as the multiple of debt system, with a small difference. As its name indicates, this "buyout" requires the student to repay a multiple of the original amount and the accrued interest at the moment the repayment takes place.

Johnstone (1972) concludes that a multiple of debt and interest "buyout" is the most appropriate alternative for implementing a mutualized ICL. In chapter 7, I conclude that it is precisely this "buyout" option that most closely resembles the financial benefits a student receives from an ICL.

7. Johnstone (1972, 69).
8. Testimony before the US Senate Subcommittee on Employment and Manpower, September 20, 1963, as reported in Dinerstein (1969).
9. Johnstone (1972, 72).
10. Panel on Educational Innovation (Jerrold Zacharias, Chairman), *Educational Opportunity Bank: A Report of the Panel on Educational Innovation to the US Commissioner of Education, the Director of the National Science Foundation, and the Special Assistant to the President for Science and Technology*, Washington, DC: US Government Printing Office, 1967.
11. US Department of Health, Education, and Welfare, *Toward a Long Range Plan for Federal Financial Support for Higher Education*, Washington, DC: US Government Printing Office, 1969.
12. For example, The Wran committee (1988) considered such an alternative, and the Dearing report contains allusions to it (see Barr, 1998).
13. See Barr's comments in chapter 8, p. 111.
14. Randall Lane, "Colsobs," *Forbes*, November 4, 1996, 44–45.
15. In the letter mentioned earlier in n. 4 from Becker to Chapman, Becker writes about HCCs: "they would be extremely valuable in promoting investments in human capital."
16. Colsobs stands for "Collateralized Students' Obligations."

17. The obstacles faced by Garg and Khan are discussed in chapter 8. Admittedly, only by surviving the long run can they prove that their idea was feasible.

18. An important point is that they decided *not* to price their contracts differently depending on gender. (See chapter 8 for a deeper discussion on similar issues.)

19. Davis and Meyer (2000).

5 How human capital contracts work

1. As my intent is to help readers understand the features of the contract, my discussion is framed in lay terms. The actual terms of the contract will look different, i.e. much more complicated.

2. The perception has to be relative to their peers, because HCC pricing will reflect the *average* expected income from a certain group of students.

3. The strong assumption here is that there is positive correlation between an individual's pre-college perception of income potential and the individual's actual income potential. Intuitively it makes sense to assume that there is such a correlation, though research confirming it would be needed.

4. See chapter 2 for details on adverse selection. The discussion in this chapter follows the same logic that Nobel Prize winner George Akerlof uses (see Akerlof, 1970).

5. Under these conditions, the percentage of income asked from the potential high- and low-income earners would be different. The process described here is analogous to the different premiums that individuals pay to obtain insurance.

6. Private interviews with Vishal Garg and Raza Khan (November 2001) and Roy Chapman (February and June 2001). Cited with their permission.

7. John's payment is kept apart from the percentage calculation because his payment estimated as a percentage of income exceeds the $80,000 cap ($1,000,000*13.3% = $133,000).

8. The problem is not insurmountable because the value of education can be inferred by estimating the value of the human capital option (HCO) embedded in the capped HCC. This measure, however, is still only indirect.

9. I argue elsewhere that one of the advantages of HCCs is precisely that they are not a financial burden when the student's income is low. They do not protect, however, against irresponsible spending on the part of the student. Although the lenders cannot predict irresponsible

behavior, the probability of distress decreases with the percentage of income committed by the student.

10. This is precisely the parameter studied when rating agencies analyze the interest coverage of a particular company. Another example in individuals is the criteria used by landlords to decide whether or not to lease a house or apartment.

11. See chapter 7 for a brief description of financial options. Appendix B (p. 175) offers a simplified method for valuing them. The exit condition is a call option because it gives the student the right to buy back the obligation he has with the investor.

12. MyRichUncle's™ Master Funding Agreement includes certain deferment conditions, such as pursuing additional education. These conditions have the same effect than the "productive period" definition.

13. The previous statement is true for diversification in any kind of asset, as Harry Markowitz proved in his famous paper "Portfolio Selection" (see Markowitz, 1952).

14. These are often cited as "unprofitable careers." The expected earnings of individuals that choose to follow these paths are certainly, on average, much smaller than those in careers such as law, medicine, or business. The cost of education in these less profitable areas is not proportionally lower, though. In many universities, the cost per credit hour is the same for all courses. A positive result of the introduction of HCCs would be the explicit recognition on the part of schools that each credit hour does not cost the same, and thus, students should be charged proportionately. With the flat rates that exist today in many schools, the literature student who needs only books, pens, and a teacher subsidizes the cost of the medical doctor, who needs much more expensive equipment and laboratories. Chapter 6 cites information regarding Australia's universities, where the cost of providing medical training is around five times higher than the cost of offering some social science courses.

15. The author thanks Hans Paris from IFC for bringing forward the notion that any asset can be securitized, as long as there is someone willing to take the first loss.

6 The case for human capital contracts

1. These failures are described in chapter 2. The main problem for students is the lack of knowledge about the return they will obtain from their investment. The main problem for investors is the lack of collateral from human capital and asymmetric information on the capabilities and intentions of the student.

2. Figure 6.1 shows only one pay-off structure for ICRS, that for HCCs. The pay-off will vary for different kinds of ICRS.

3. The "default zone" is simplified here for exposition purposes. In a real case, the "default zone" will be larger, since students will presumably use their income to cover their basic necessities before taking care of loan payments.

4. This can be seen directly in appendix A, where the valuation of HCCs is discussed.

5. Assuming that post-graduate earnings' expectations reflect the quality of the preparation of students who graduate from a particular university.

6. The income growth function $(G(t))$ might also be a function of the school attended. In that case, costs at a particular school have to be compared with the expected starting income and its growth.

7. Eventually, to keep the liberty and variety of options available for students in universities, each different course should be charged according to its cost. Whereas an exact costing is impossible, there are some clear differences that call for different pricing, such as the use of laboratories and specialized materials.

8. This is an externality, or a "neighbor" effect.

9. MyRichUncle℠ was, to the author's knowledge, the only venture offering HCCs in 2001. More recently, Lumni and Career Concept have financed students using HCCs in Chile and Germany, respectively.

10. MyRichUncle's℠ Master Agreement can be found on the company's web page. The exact location at the time this book was written was www.myrichuncle.com/Images/HowItWks/Terms/SampleMFA.pdf.

7 Human capital options

1. The use of options to value contingent claims starts with Black and Sholes' original paper, "The Pricing of Options and Corporate Liabilities" (1973).

2. Options have been used to value government guarantees (see Mody, 1996), as those given to student loans. Here the analysis is made for ICLs.

3. The value of the option will depend on the value of the underlying asset. This is the reason why options are a *derivative* security: they *derive* their value from another asset.

4. What is a favorable or unfavorable change in value depends on the nature of the option. If the option is a call option, then increases in the value of the underlying asset are favorable. On the other hand, if the option is a put option, then falls in the value of the underlying asset are favorable.

5. The example outlined below assumes that the income of the individual can be accurately determined. For instance, it could be defined as the Gross Income that appears in the individual's tax declaration.
6. A discussion of what the appropriate rate can be is found in chapter 1.
7. In all the graphs that follow in this chapter, positive values are payments received by the student, and negative values are payments made by the student. This convention is kept through all of them to be consistent.
8. This equivalency is a special case of what is known in finance as the "put-call parity."
9. See Johnstone (2001a) and Barr (2001).
10. The implementation of Australia's ICLs and Yale's TPP is studied in more detail in chapter 9.
11. The extra charge is always a maximum. An individual's obligation may finish before if the "pooled" loan is repaid completely before the individual pays the maximum amount.
12. Australia's HECS program does this indirectly, though for a different purpose, by offering a discount on university fees to those who pay upon enrollment. Students who take the ICL have to pay back an amount higher than what they would have to pay if they used a private loan to pay for the discounted fee.
13. The use of options to value "insurance" is found in Merton (1977).

8 Hurdles in the implementation of human capital contracts

1. This criterion fits well the classic definition of liberty (for instance, see Hayek, 1960, ch. I, 11).
2. For an interesting discussion of differences on returns to education obtained by groups of individuals other than white males in the United States, see Becker (1993, ch. VIII).
3. Some industries offer different prices to different groups of people based on their risk profiles. This is particularly true in the insurance industry.
4. Friedman (1962, 218).
5. Friedman (1962, 103).
6. This view is challenged by Garg and Khan of MyRichUncle.[TM] (See chapter 5.)
7. For the particular concerns of a US investor, see Palacios (2002).
8. The investor is indirectly affected by the double taxation because the contract is much less attractive for the student, creating pressure on investors to lower the percentage of income they can ask per dollar provided.

9. For example, tax authorities should state whether or not, and under what conditions, investors can depreciate their investment.

10. Technically, students are selling a fraction of their future income. Thus, they should not be taxed on it. Following the same logic, they should be taxed for the proceeds they obtain when they sell it. Investors, on the other hand, are making an investment and expecting a future stream of cash flows from it. Investments should be depreciated for a period of time equal to the life of the asset.

11. I am indebted to Raza Khan, co-founder of MyRichUncle™, for raising the idea that being debt-free may change students' attitudes towards risk.

12. Gary Becker writes in *Human Capital* (1993) about small manufacturing investments as bearing comparable risks to education investments. The returns on the manufacturing assets at the time he originally wrote (1964), were estimated at around 8 percent. Psacharopoulos (1994) uses 8.7 percent. Current returns to education are estimated to be higher and thus provide an investment opportunity.

13. There will always be a small fraction of defaults related to financial distress induced by an individual's irresponsible spending habits.

14. Defaults on first-year payments in federally guaranteed student loans fell from 22.6 percent in 1990 to 6.9 percent in 1998. *Source:* Department of Education statistics www.ed.gov/offices/OSFAP/defaultmanagement/defaultrates.html

15. Placing conditions for paying less than the "capped amount" of an HCC that is also an ICL, as discussed in chapter 5, goes in the same direction as the one Johnstone proposes for implementing ICLs in countries with unreliable tax authorities or large informal sectors (see Johnstone and Aemero, 2001).

16. Barr analyzes the possible impact of emigration for an ICL scheme he proposed for the UK, concluding that the impact should not be significant (see Barr, 1989, ch. 5).

17. Barr (2001, ch. 14, section 2).

18. Barr (2001, 234).

19. In Chile's case, payments go to private pension funds; in Australia, although payments still go to a national account, they are available only for higher education.

20. Australia's experience estimates collection costs around 0.5 percent (Chapman and Nicholls, 2002).

21. Assuming that his borrowing cost reflects the risk of the investments he is making.

9 Lessons from the implementation of income-contingent loans

1. The author thanks Mort Engstrom for his aid in the preparation of this section. Mr. Engstrom provided relevant information and generously participated in a workshop organized by the Batten Institute on HCCs. Mr. Engstrom is director of capital management of Yale University, and was directly involved in analyzing the results of Yale's income-contingent repayment plan more than twenty years after its implementation.

2. The information on this section comes from Yale's Tuition Postponement Program brochures (1971). For detailed discussions and descriptions see Johnstone (1972). Hartman (1972) analyzes the distribution effects of ICLs and of Yale's program in particular. Nerlove (1975) analyzes some of the problems faced in the implementation of the program.

3. ICLs where high-income earners subsidize low-income earners are known as "mutualized" loans.

4. See Bulkeley (1999).

5. As will be discussed later in this chapter, Australia's HECS program also has long repayment periods. The reaction of the public to this repayment schedule is still not evident because the program was implemented only in 1989. This will be a relevant concern for those running the HECS program during the coming decades.

6. This paradigm is widely accepted in the corporate world. Corporations are willing to enter into very long-term obligations to finance long-term projects.

7. Notice that this reaction is purely psychological, as students are really adjusting their payments to their capacity to pay.

8. In the Australian case explored below, the subsidy comes directly from the government.

9. The variation of the implicit interest rate with the repayment period is also discussed below in the Australian HECS program.

10. This is a manifestation of opportunism. Frequently, when a contract is struck in the face of uncertainty, the party that ends up with a bad deal will try to rescind their obligations.

11. This contrasts with other programs where group responsibility is the basis of repayment, such as micro-lending. In this case, all debtors live in the same community and, thus, there are communal mechanisms for sanctioning those who do not pay. Because Yale's graduates live all over the world, community pressure is not an important factor for them.

12. The author thanks Bruce Chapman for providing most of the relevant information for this chapter and for the time given during a telephone interview. Most of the information presented here can be found in Chapman (1997, 1999). Other comments and ideas come from a telephone interview made by the author in July 2001.

13. Edwards, Howard and Miller (2002) give a very interesting account of the process that eventually led to the creation of HECS. Edwards was part of the Wran committee, which recommended the introduction of HECS in its 1988 report.

14. For example, Barr (1998) includes this concern as an issue in the implementation of ICLs in the UK.

15. Although, as long as the fund's income remains a fraction of the higher-education costs paid from taxes, the "exclusive use" of the funds remains only an accounting reality.

16. Also known as "externalities" or "spillover effects." This argument was presented in chapter 2 when explaining the market failure in financing education.

17. See Chapman (1997).

18. As discussed above, Yale did have a real interest rate and after twenty-five years students complained that the system was flawed because of the significant increase in the nominal amount of their loan.

19. Quoted by Chapman (1997).

20. In general, this conclusion will always be true as long as the rate that reflects the risk on the loan is *higher* than the interest rate charged on the loan.

21. New Zealand's experience, discussed below, shows that it is not always possible to charge a market interest rate.

22. Using the state to collect payments can be efficient, in theory, for any kind of loan, regardless of whether it is income-contingent or not. However, there are reasons for restraining the tax collection system from collecting any kind of payment. These were discussed in chapter 8.

23. The University Credit is one of several programs that Chile's government uses to fund higher education Among the other programs are direct transfers to universities, vouchers paid to schools depending on the quality of students they enroll, other subsidized loans (Crédito Corfo), grants, and scholarships.

24. This number reflects collection for other types of loans as well, so the collection amount for only the income-contingent ones could be different.

10 Government-driven implementation of human capital contracts

1. In Chile's case, payments go to private pension funds; in Australia, although payments still go to a national account, they are available only for higher education.
2. Australia's experience estimates collection costs around 0.5 percent. (See Chapter 9.)
3. For instance, individuals in Chile have different percentages of income withheld, depending on the pension fund they are affiliated with; in Australia, the percentage of income retained for HECS is a function of the individual's income.
4. Governments face similar concerns when trying to sell student debt.
5. Mentioned in personal conversation with the author. Quoted with his permission.
6. Such as Colombia's SENA contribution tax.
7. For instance, government employees might still have other sources of income that are difficult to track.
8. See chapter 1.
9. Assuming constant tax regulations.
10. This example starts with public schools because government is funding them already. A more complex scheme is described later in this chapter to include private schools.
11. Such a system also opens the possibility for the creation of independent quality assessment institutions that would guide the decisions of investors. The service that these institutions would provide is analogous to that provided by rating agencies such as Standard & Poor's or Moody's. By assessing the overall quality of schools, "education rating agencies" would make valuable information available for investors (and, arguably, for students).
12. There are several ways to determine which students each investor finances. The easiest to implement is to pool each class together and give each investor a share of the percentage of income the whole class gives back. For example, in the previous example bidder 1 finances 600 students that represent 60 percent of the class (school A has 1,000 available spaces) and thus is entitled to 6 percent of 60 percent of the class, or (6 percent × 60 percent), 3.6 percent of the class' income. Other alternatives include matching the best bid with a ranking of students, or having investors choose individually. These two options would add complexity to the system as well as open opportunities for arbitrariness in the selection, and thus are not considered further here.

13. This particular finance rule urges investors to hedge against rein-vestment or refinancing risk. If the life of the asset is shorter than the life of the liability, the investor faces the risk of not finding an-other investment that can pay for the cost of the remaining life of the liability. If the life of the liability is shorter than the life of the asset, the investor faces the risk of not finding a favorable rate at which to obtain additional funds to cover the remaining life of the asset.

14. Colombia's monthly minimum salary in 2001 was 286,000 Colombian pesos. The monthly income threshold for starting to pay income tax is 1,401,000 Colombian pesos, or 4.9 times the minimum monthly wage. The following table shows the distribution of income in Colombia in 1999.

Income level	Households	% of total
Less than 1 minimum wage	6,596,390	49.9
Between 1 and 2 times minimum wage	4,357,014	33.0
Between 2 and 3 times minimum wage	1,062,986	8.0
Between 3 and 4 times minimum wage	356,827	2.7
Between 4 and 5 times minimum wage	246,934	1.9
Between 5 and 6 times minimum wage	147,420	1.1
More than 6 times minimum wage	440,526	3.3
TOTAL	13,208,097	100.0

Source: DANE Statistics, www.dane.gov.co.

11 Conclusion

1. The author thanks Nicholas Barr for suggesting the inclusion of this relevant point.
2. Friedman (1962, 107).

Appendix A

1. This section considers only HCCs without caps. An HCC with a cap can always be valued as a combination of a loan and an option; the subject of chapter 7 and appendix B.
2. This analysis leaves out the error term, as our goal here is to derive an average value at which HCCs would be offered. Incorporating the variability in income is necessary for a risk analysis of an investment in an HCC.

Appendix B

1. Students with the same amount of total income during the life of the contract do not necessarily pay the same because those who take longer to pay back the loan receive a higher subsidy than those who pay faster. This raises fairness concerns, since individuals with the same present value of income would pay different amounts for their education.
2. For an analysis of this kind of mutualized ICL see (Johnstone, 1972).
3. Figure B.3 can also have the same shortcomings as figure B.2: students with the same present value income might pay more or less, depending on the timing of their income.
4. The Black–Scholes equation for valuing options can be found in any basic finance text. For example, see Breaely and Myers (2000, 606).
5. Following the argument presented so far, the option in an ICL is a put. However, combining a call and an HCC produces the same financial results.

Appendix D

1. See Mincer's (1974) discussion on why it is preferable to use experience rather than age to estimate earnings. Age is used when there is no direct information on experience.
2. The equation has the same form, but h is replaced by $h-2Ag$.
3. *Source*: Banco de La República, Colombia's central bank. www.banrep. gov.co/economia.
4. www.dane.gov.co/Informacion_Estadistica/Estadisticas/Fuerza_de_ Trabajo/Encuesta_Nacional_de_Hogares/Tasa_de_Desempleo/ tasadesetasa_de_desempleo1.html.
5. Núñez excludes from the informal sector those individuals who are affiliated to the social security system. This is the relevant figure for HCCs because income can be determined from those affiliated to the social security system.
6. *Source*: Standard & Poor's, http://www.standardandpoors.com/ RatingsActions/RatingsLists/ Sovereigns/SovereignsRatingsList.html.
7. *Source*: Citibank Colombia, Daily indicator report, November 9, 2001. bps is basis points.
8. On a pure economic analysis, the student should be willing to pay a much higher percentage, since the difference in earnings between an individual with high-school education and an individual with five additional years of education is 67 percent. However, individuals raise their consumption as their permanent income increases and the difference

in earnings will not be available to pay for higher education financing. Asking a high percentage of a student's income will also increase moral hazard and will act as a disincentive for working.

9. Assuming real fees remain constant and discounting by 10 percent.
10. This assumption is reasonable considering that families are expected to survive with it. However, Ziderman and Albrecht (1995, 38) use a figure that for 1989 was, at best, 19 percent without including forgone earnings. Their figures might not be comparable since the tuition costs used in this example are estimated in 2000 and their calculations were estimated with 1989 data.

References

Akerlof, George, 1970. "The Market for Lemons: Quality Uncertainty and the Market Mechanism," *Quarterly Journal of Economics*, 84(3), 488–500

Albrecht, Douglas and Ziderman, Adrian, 1991. "Deferred Cost Recovery for Higher Education: Student Loan Programs in Developing Countries," *World Bank Discussion Papers*, 137, Washington, DC, World Bank

Aristotle, 1992. *The Politics*, trans. T. A. Sinclair. Harmondsworth, Penguin Books

Arrow, Kenneth J., 1971. *Essays in the Theory of Risk-Bearing*. Chicago, Markham

Azariadis C., and Drazen, Alan, 1990. "Threshold Externalities in Economic Development," *Quarterly Journal of Economics*, 105(2), 501–526

Barr, Nicholas, 1987. *The Economics of the Welfare State*. Stanford, Stanford University Press

1989. *Student Loans, The Next Steps*. Aberdeen, Aberdeen University Press for the David Hume Institute, and the Suntory-Toyota International Centre for Economics and Related Disciplines, London School of Economics

1998. "The Dearing Report and the Government's Response: A Critique," *The Political Quarterly*, 69(1)

2001. *The Welfare State as Piggy Bank: Information, Risk, Uncertainty, and the Role of the State*. Oxford, Oxford University Press

Becker, Gary, 1993. *Human Capital, A Theoretical and Empirical Analysis, with Special Reference to Education*, 3rd edn. Chicago, Chicago University Press

Black, Fischer and Scholes, Myron, 1973. "The Pricing of Options and Corporate Liabilities," *Journal of Political Economy*, 81(3), 637–654

Blackburn, McKinley and Neumark, David, 1995. "Are OLS Estimates of the Return to Schooling Biased Downward? Another Look," *Review of Economics and Statistics*, 77(2), 217–230

Blaug, Mark, 1970. *An Introduction to the Economics of Education*. London, Allen Lane

Breaely, Richard and Myers, Stewart, 2000. *Principles of Corporate Finance*, 6th edition. Boston, McGraw-Hill

Bulkeley, William, 1999. "Old Blues: Some Alumni of Yale Say That They Owe College a Lasting Debt – Plan Has Them Remitting A Share of Their Income Decades After Graduation – "Noble Experiment" Gone Awry," *The Wall Street Journal*, February 23, A1

Camhi, Rosita and Latnt, Rosana, 2000. "Evaluación del Sistema de Ayudas Estudiantiles a la Educación Superior," *Informe Social*, Libertad y Desarrollo, Santiago de Chile

Chapman, Bruce, 1997. "Conceptual Issues and the Australian Experience with Income Contingent Charges for Higher Education," *Economic Journal*, 107(442), 738–752

   1999. "Reform of Ethiopian Higher Education Financing: Conceptual and Policy Issues," World Bank, Economics of Education Thematic Group, Washington DC

Chapman, Bruce and Nicholls, Jane, 2002. "Income Contingent Loans for Higher Education: Implementation Issues for Developing Countries," Australian National University, mimeo

Chiswick, Barry, 1997. "Interpreting the Coefficient of Schooling in the Human Capital Earnings Function," World Bank Working Papers, 1790

Colclough, Christopher, 1990. "Raising Additional Resources for Education in Developing Countries: Are Graduate Payroll Taxes Superior to Student Loans?," *International Journal of Educational Development*, 10(2/3), 169–180

Committee on Higher Education Financing, 1998. *Report of the Committee on Higher Education Funding* (Wran report). Canberra, Australian Government Publishing Service

Davis, Stan and Meyer, Christopher, 2000. *Future Wealth*. Boston, Harvard Business School Press

Dinerstein, Rita, 1967. "Long-Term Student Loans: Selected Proposals for Repayment Based on 'Ability to Repay,'" Washington, DC: The Library of Congress Legislative Reference Service, October 31

Edwards, Meredith with Howard, Cosmo and Miller, Robin, 2001. *Social Policy, Public Policy: From Problem to Practice*. Crows Nest,   Allen & Unwin

Friedman, Milton, 1955. "The Role of Government in Education," in R. A. Solow (ed.), *Economics and the Public Interest*. Piscataway, Rutgers University Press

   1962. *Capitalism and Freedom*. Chicago, Chicago University Press

Friedman, Milton and Kuznets, Simon Smith, 1945. *Income From Independent Professional Practice*. New York, National Bureau of Economic Research

Glennerster, Howard, Merrett, Stephen and Wilson, Grail, 1968. "A Graduate Tax," *Higher Education Review*, 1(1)

Griliches, Zvi, 1977. "Estimating the Returns to Schooling: Some Econometric Problems," *Econometrica*, 45(1), 1–22

Harding, Ann, 1993. "Lifetime Repayment Patterns for HECS and AUSTUDY Loans," Discussion Paper, 1, National Center for Social and Economic Modelling, Faculty of Management, Canberra University

1995. "Financing Higher Education: An Assessment of Income-Contingent Loan Options and Repayment Patterns over the Life Cycle," *Education Economics*, 3, 173–203

Hartman, Robert, 1972. "Equity Implications of State Tuition Policy and Student Loans," *Journal of Political Economy*, 80(3), part II, S142–S171

Hayek, Frederic, 1960. *The Constitution of Liberty*. Chicago, Chicago University Press

Johnstone, Bruce, 1972. *New Patterns for College Lending: Income-Contingent Loans*. New York and London, Columbia University Press

2001. "The Economics and Politics of Income Contingent Repayment Plans," paper found at Johnstone's web page at the University of Buffalo, www.gse.buffalo.edu/FAS/Johnston/Loans.html

Johnstone, Bruce and Aemero, Abebayehu, 2001. "The Applicability for Developing Countries of Income-Contingent Loans or Graduate Taxes, with Special Consideration of an Australian HECS-Type Income-Contingent Loan Program for Ethiopia," available through the International Comparative Higher Education Finance and Accessibility Project, University of Buffalo Center for Comparative and Global Studies in Education, www.gse.buffalo.edu/org/IntHigherEdFinance

Killingworth, Charles C., 1967. "How to Pay for Higher Education," presidential address at the Economics Society of Michigan, Ann Arbor, March 17

Lane, Randall, 1996. "Colsobs," *Forbes*, November 4, 44–45

Leiva, Alicia, 2002. "El financiamiento estudiantil para la educación superior," *Colección Ideas*, 3(21), Santiago, Fundación Chile21

López, Hugo, 2001. "La Financiación de la Educación Superior. Necesidad de un Sistema de Crédito Estudiantil y Alternativas para su Montaje," paper presented at "La educación superior, desafío global y respuesta nacional," Universidad de los Andes. Bogotá

Markowitz, Harry, 1952. "Portfolio Selection," *Journal of Finance*, 7(1), 77–91

Marshall, Alfred, 1956/1890. *Principles of Economics: An Introductory Volume*, 8th edn. London, Macmillan

Merton, Robert C., 1977. "An Analytic Derivation of the Cost of Deposit Insurance and Loan Guarantees: An Application of Modern Option Pricing Theory," *Journal of Banking and Finance*, 1(1), 3–11

  1998. "Applications of Option-Pricing Theory: Twenty-Five Years Later," *American Economic Review*, 88(3), 323–349

Mincer, Jacob, 1974. *Schooling, Experience and Earnings*. New York, Columbia University Press

Mody, Ashoka, 1996. "Valuing and Accounting for Loan Guarantees," *World Bank Research Observer*, 11(1), 119–142

Moretti, Enrico, 2002. "Estimating the Social Return to Higher Education: Evidence From Longitudinal and Repeated Cross-Sectional Data," National Bureau of Economic Research Working Papers, 3(89)

Mulligan, Casey, 1999. "Galton Versus the Human Capital Approach to Inheritance," *Journal of Political Economy*, 107(6), part 2, "Symposium on the Economic Analysis of Social Behavior in Honor of Gary S. Becker," S184–S224

Nerlove, Marc, 1972. "On Tuition and the Costs of Higher Education: Prolegomena to a Conceptual Framework," *Journal of Political Economy*, 80(3), part II, S178–S218

  1975. "Some Problems in the Use of Income-Contingent Loans for the Finance of Higher Education," *Journal of Political Economy*, 83(1), 157–183

Núñez, Jairo, 2000. "Empleo Informal y Evasión Fiscal en Colombia," paper financed by the Inter-American Development Bank

Núñez, Jairo and Sánchez, Fabio, 2000. "A Dynamic Analysis of Household Decision Making in Urban Colombia, 1976–1998," research project presented to the Inter-American Development Bank

Oosterbeek, Hessel, 1998. "Innovative Ways to Finance Education and Their Relation to Lifelong Learning," *Education Economics*, 9(3), 219–251

Palacios, Miguel, 2002. "Human Capital Contracts: 'Equity-Like' Instruments for Financing Higher Education," *Policy Analysis Paper*, 492. Washington, DC, The Cato Institute

Psacharopoulos, George, 1994. "Returns to Investments in Education: A Global Update," *World Development*, 22(9), 1325–1343

Psacharopoulos, G., Tan, J.-P. and Jiménez, E., 1986. *Financing Education in Developing Countries: An Exploration of Policy Options*. Washington, DC, World Bank

Reuterberg, Sven, 1990. "Student Financial Aid in Sweden," *Higher Education Policy*, 3(3), 33–38

Tehlado, Pedro and Silva, Pedro, 2001. "Is There a Return–Risk Link in Education?," *Institute for the Study of Labor (IZA)*, Discussion Paper, 321

Thurow, Lester C., 1996. *The Future of Capitalism: How Today's Economic Forces Shape Tomorrow's World*. New York, William Morrow and Co., Inc.

Wran report, 1998. *See* Committee on Higher Education Financing

Yale University, 1971. "1971–1972 Tuition Postponement Option Plan," brochures, New Haven, CT

Ziderman, Adrian and Albrecht, Douglas, 1995. *Financing Universities in Developing Countries*. Washington, DC, Falmer Press

Index